Smuggling
in
East Anglia
1700–1840

Smuggling
in
East Anglia
1700–1840

STAN JARVIS

COUNTRYSIDE BOOKS

NEWBURY, BERKSHIRE

FIRST PUBLISHED 1987
© Stan Jarvis 1987

Reprinted 1990

ISBN 0 905392 86 8

The cover illustration *Beach Landing*
is from a drawing by Edward Dowden

Produced through MRM Associates Ltd., Reading
Typeset by Acorn Bookwork, Salisbury
Printed in England by J. W. Arrowsmith, Bristol
Printed on acid-free paper

Contents

Acknowledgements	*6*
Introduction	*7*
1. How it Began	*11*
2. The Impact on East Anglia	*31*
3. From the Thames to the Blackwater	*45*
4. From the Colne to the Stour	*65*
5. From the Orwell to the Alde	*85*
6. From the Alde to the Yare	*103*
7. From the Yare to Stiffkey	*131*
8. From Stiffkey to King's Lynn	*147*
Bibliography	*169*
Index	*171*

Acknowledgements

Many people have helped me in the course of research for this work. At the outset Mr Hervey Benham, the well-known author, gave advice and encouragement. Graham Smith, Librarian and Archivist of H.M. Customs and Excise guided me through the original records and the books at King's Beam House, and gave me the benefit of his wide knowledge of his subject as displayed in the books he has written on the Service. Mr A. Rodway and Sally Faulkner welcomed me to the King's Lynn Custom House and made my search through their old records a positive pleasure.

The Archivists and their staff in the Record Offices of Essex, Suffolk and Norfolk have patiently answered my letters and introduced me to their repositories. The staff of the Chelmsford Library have gone beyond the call of duty in providing recondite material for loan.

My wife Hazel, companion on all my journeys, has helped in the research and inspired me afresh when the task seemed almost too much. Many friends, to numerous to be individually acknowledged, have offered helpful points. Lastly I would thank Nicholas Battle for the trust he has shown in me to produce this book.

Introduction

'"Smugglers," said Father William, "th' Lord love an' keep ye! I knows a might about they. Do ye plenish me fire an' draw th' curtain, an' I'll tell ye 'bout 'em."' So S. L. Bensusan started a chapter of *A Countryside Chronicle*, written in 1907. Born in 1872, Bensusan was a journalist and well-known music critic who, coming to live in Essex, was captivated by the county and its characters, particularly those of the marshlands and the remote villages of the Dengie Hundred. The material for his books, essentially fictional chronicles of rural life, was gathered from real-life conversations and observations he heard and made in the pub, on the road, in the fields and on the quay. Father William was a composite of all the old men who regaled him with the stories of their lives, and the tales their grandfathers told them. Handed-down recollections of distant days of smuggling came readily to their lips, and Bensusan put them into Father William's mouth: '"If ther' was 'arf th' pluck ther' used to be when I wor a lad, they'd be out wi' th' boats, an ye'd see some o' they big-sail'd luggers a-turnin' in fr' th' main, an' all th' stuff o'erboard down be Cripple's Creek, an' th' light a-shinin', an' th' hosses a-gallopin', an' fook lookin' out o' th' winders, though they dussent never show n' lights. Ah, they was a foine set o' min an' we shaint see th' likes o' they in these parts again."'

In reality smuggling was an occupation far removed from the romance of Father William's handed-down, nostalgic folklore. It was an activity born of greed and need. Many of the items on which heavy duty was payable were luxury goods — even tea and coffee were classed as such in the 18th century. It was greed for them, and for the status their possession conferred upon people of polite society, that created the demand which the smugglers, greedy for their own financial gain,

7

could meet, albeit at great risk. But there was also need: that of the poverty-stricken labourers. For such people a night assisting the smugglers yielded either a bellyful of temporary euphoria from a cask of gin or brandy, or a payment which made the return from regular and honest labour seem laughable.

Such a night was not always blessed by the moonlight, balmy breezes and calm waters of popular fiction. A landing on the beach at any time from September right through to March could be a cold, wet, troublesome, tiring and really dangerous business. There was also another side to the coin; it should be remembered that public servants such as the Riding Officers and the crews of the Revenue cutters were enduring nights of equal discomfort, and indeed risking their lives as they faced the hazards of stormy weather and the weapons of the smugglers they attempted to capture.

Such was the attraction of cut-price liquor and fancy goods, as well as a hundred and one items in daily use, that by the 18th century smuggling had become a very profitable, highly-organised business. Many gang leaders lived on the Continent so they could deal direct with their regular suppliers. The goods were taken to certain Continental ports where they were loaded aboard ships specially built at those ports for the purpose. Large sums were invested in these trips, and the goods were landed on the English coast in vast quantities under armed guard; these men, sharing in the profits, would fiercely resist any attempt to seize the contraband or capture the smugglers.

The geography of the coastline was a major influence on the scale of smuggling operations, and the methods used by the smugglers. In those days the east coast from Southend-on-Sea to King's Lynn was bleak and lonely, with miles of remote shores, saltings, mudflats and sandbanks where contraband could be run ashore undetected, and carried by horses and carts from the sea wall to the high road. The swirling tide soon removed the evidence of the smugglers' footprints and the tracks of their unshod horses.

Different methods evolved to suit the lie of the land and the ways of the sea on these sandbank-strewn shallows of East Anglia. For example, sinking cargoes in the shallower waters of estuaries and creeks, to be picked up later, was a very popular technique. It was often employed by crews of the packet boats as they sailed into Harwich, but it was used on a far larger scale by the professional smugglers, many of which had 'tub-boats' specially built to certain specifications to accommodate tubs and waterproofed packets weighted for dropping over the side at an agreed, marked spot.

Although there was less violence on the east coast than on the Kent and Sussex shores, there were some desperate encounters. No smuggler who had got a big cargo ashore would wish to have all his work put at nothing by the Revenue men, and if a large group of smugglers was challenged by an inferior force they would fight, and often win. Yet the Revenue men persevered, became better organised, and finally put most of the big-time smugglers out of business.

Even so, smuggling still continues today, and the east coast's nearness to the Continent has encouraged another class of opportunist: the man who makes use of every form of modern transport to deal in more dangerous and distasteful contraband such as drugs, arms and even illegal immigrants. Father William would not have approved.

East Anglia: showing major places associated with the smuggling trade.

1
How it Began

Dr Samuel Johnson, famous for the dictionary he compiled which was first published in 1755, defined a smuggler as 'A wretch who, in defiance of justice and the laws, imports or exports goods either contraband or without payment of the customs.' But Boswell, his biographer, tells us that the worthy doctor also said of his addiction to tea that he was 'a hardened and shameless tea drinker . . . whose kettle has scarcely time to cool'. It is more than likely that his friend Mrs Thrale looked for a bargain when she came to buy the tea he so much enjoyed, and she may well have known of a smuggler's agent who could get tea a little cheaper, no questions asked. In such small, domestic ways Johnson, and thousands like him, unwittingly supported a trade which had flourished since the imposition of the first customs duty.

For centuries before Johnson's time England's rulers had the power to raise money in the form of a tax on goods entering or leaving the country. This was an important slice of the cake of national income: a constant flow of cash upon which the king and his advisers could rely. But it is human nature to look for a bargain, a price reduction, and from the earliest times smugglers took advantage of this by bringing in goods without paying the tax.

The collection of this tax was in any case very complicated. The nature of goods imported and exported was constantly changing. For instance, taxes were imposed on the various materials used in the ever-changing fashions of dress. The levels of tax on every commodity also had to be listed, reviewed and revised as necessary in the light of the sum they produced. The job was made easier by restricting the import and export of goods to specified, recognised ports, in each of which a Custom House was established. Specially-appointed officers working from the Custom House could supervise the loading and unloading of goods to see that the appropriate 'duty' was paid. The word itself demonstrates the antiquity of the practice of raising revenue in this way, for it is derived from the Anglo-French of the Normans, and means something that is owing – in this case to the Crown.

Another tax, Excise Duty, was introduced during the English Civil War, when enormous additional sums were required to offset the terrible drain on the economy of such an armed struggle. A wide range of manufactured items, even as homely as tallow candles, were subject to this tax. It has persisted to this day as Value Added Tax. When such items were exported, Revenue Tax had to be paid as well – and both taxes were applied to goods entering the country. So it was that many goods, essential or luxurious, could cost the consumer up to three times their original price. Smugglers were quickly on the scene to exploit this situation and make a very good living from it.

Tax was also used as a means of regulating trade. Such a tax was imposed in 1275, when English cloth-makers were having a hard time because their product was being imitated and under-sold by foreign weavers who had the nerve to import English wool for the purpose. Once the export tax had raised the price of English wool, smugglers could reap a good return on a cross-channel voyage with an illicit cargo of sacks of wool. Enormous quantities of that wool were produced from the sheep kept in vast flocks throughout East Anglia from Norman times onwards, where to quote Charles Harper's *Smugglers* of 1909 'the low, muddy shores and ramifying creeks of Essex and the sandy, coastwise warrens of Suffolk, Norfolk and Lincolnshire, very sparsely inhabited, offered their own peculiar facilities for the shy and secretive trade'.

There are references from as far back as the middle of the 14th century to this illegal export of English wool and woollen cloth, and the trade continued well into the 18th century. The number of packs of wool spirited abroad from Kent and Sussex in the year 1700 has been estimated at 150,000. This activity, carried out at night when the owl was abroad on its own nefarious business, came to be called 'owling'. It was a part of daily life for many East Anglian fishermen, and the proceeds

Secluded creeks, like this one at Kirby-le-Soken were ideal for the secret unloading of contraband cargo.

made a very welcome addition to the precarious income from fishing which in those days was essentially a seasonal occupation. Smuggling runs helped to fill winter's 'hungry gap'.

The earliest record found of 'owling' is in the Fine Rolls of Edward III. On 26 January 1361 there was sent an 'Order to Reynoldde Sholdham, searcher of the king's forfeitures in the water of the Thames, as well in the port of London as elsewhere in the county of Essex – on a report from him that, having found by inquisition that William de Okele of Reyle [probably Ray Island near West Mersea] and Thomas his brother, had 4 sarplars [half sacks] of wool at Bradewell in the house of John Dounyng on the seashore, which they would have shipped in a certain small ship near the said house if the ship had not been arrested by William de Hynton, late the king's searcher, as forfeit to the king because it was laden with uncustomed wools, he arrested the said sarplars as forfeit, and that the wools are still kept under arrest – to release the said

13

sarplars from arrest, if they were arrested in the above account and no other, and to deliver them to William and Thomas; as the said William and Thomas have paid the king 40s., and have represented that the wool was found lying in the house without sarplars and sacks, and was not placed there for shipment, and that they are not found guilty of any evil intent in the matter. And the 40s. have been paid in the hanaper.' The 'hanaper' was a former department of the Chancery.

Despite the tortuous language this is clear evidence of smuggling in Essex more than 600 years ago, to evade the tax on the export of wool. The tax was imposed during the reign of Edward I, and it was he who introduced the impressive 'King's Beams': huge scales for weighing the wool which were set up at every Custom House in the country. The address of the headquarters of H.M. Customs & Excise is still shown as King's Beam House in the City of London.

The duty on wool was increased over the years until it was decided that the time had come to enforce a complete ban on its export in order to protect and encourage the English weaving industry. From 1662, evasion of this ban was considered serious enough to merit capital punishment.

In these circumstances there were plenty of merchants on the Continent who were prepared to offer a good price for English wool. Since fishermen risked their lives at sea every time they set sail, they were undeterred by the death penalty and loaded up with wool. But then the centre of weaving moved from the south-east to the north, new materials were introduced and the value of wool fell. Eventually the tax was reduced and the 'owling' ceased.

By 1700, when Britain was a military and sea power to be reckoned with, the government was exercised to find the money to meet the ever-increasing expense of defending its interests. At the same time, many merchants were making use of the trade routes protected by British soldiers and sailors to import luxury goods from all over the world, and becoming very rich in the process. It seemed obvious that the new, growing class of better-off people who could afford these luxuries could also afford to pay a little extra in the form of a tax to subsidise the protection of the trade routes. By 1760 a list of such luxuries had been established, with 800 items on

which importers, be they merchants or merely travellers, had to pay customs duty at the port of entry. During the next 50 years another 1300 items were added to the list. In view of this it is little wonder that the latter part of the 18th century was a golden age for smugglers. Their patrons must have been happy too, for the smuggled, untaxed goods were cheaper than legitimate imports.

The goods affected were of the widest range, picked by the Government of the day as offering the best returns to the Treasury. They included all the details of dress, the extravagances of food and drink, and the indulgences of tobacco and snuff. Even small items, from playing cards to coffin nails, came under the watchful eye of the Customs officer. There were so many classes of goods on which swingeing taxes were laid that the merchants claimed that the very principle of free trade was effectively denied them. The smugglers took up their cry and termed themselves Free Traders – gaining some admiration for their daring and for the 'service' they performed.

The fact that smuggled luxury goods cost less meant that those with sufficient money to buy them – the richer people of the area, responsible for law and order and the proper administration of local government – often turned a blind eye to the figures who slipped along in the darkness, leaving gin or lace or what-you-will by the gate. Even the vicar could be involved. Parson Woodforde, vicar of Weston Longville, near Norwich, in the late 18th century, enters in his diary for 15 September 1792 'Had a Tub of Rum brought me this Evening.' On 17 September he writes 'I got up very early this Morning and was very busy all the Morn' in very necessary business.' The editor of the 1927 edition of his diary observes 'Parson Woodforde was presumably busy in hiding, perhaps even burying, his smuggled rum. We share his anxiety for, by clause xxii of 19 Geo. III, c. 69, he was liable to a forfeit of £10 for each offence of buying smuggled goods, while the village blacksmith, as supplier, was liable to a fine of £50. Moreover, the Act deliberately encouraged the odious practice of "informing" because it provided that if the seller informed against the buyer within twenty days, and before any information had been laid against himself, he would be forgiven his own offence.'

On 20 October 1792 the parson enters 'To my Blacksmith,

Parson Woodforde, whose household diaries reveal that smuggling was both widespread and commonplace in the 18th century.

Jno. Buck, my Annual Little Bill for Divers Matters done for me pd. him 1.13.3.' Two days later he wrote 'Bottled off my Gin received last night.' It was only ten days before this that John Buck was fined following the discovery of a tub of gin in his house by the Excise officers.

16   In the process of editing Parson Woodforde's diary John

Beresford noted that on 16 January 1777 the parson paid 'Richard Andrews a Smuggler' £1.5s.6d. for a pound of tea and three silk India handkerchiefs, explaining in a footnote 'Smuggling was a commonplace of 18th-century life, and was due entirely to high Protection . . . In England, before Pitt took the whole business in hand from 1784 onwards, smuggling was carried on on a scale which was simply colossal. The annual defalcation of the revenue was estimated at £2,000,000 out of a total revenue of £12,500,000. Whole fleets of ships and armies of persons were engaged in the smuggling business.' Pitt himself has been quoted as saying that although 13 million pounds of tea were consumed in a year in this country, duty was paid on only 5½ million. Characteristically, Pitt set about improving this situation. He greatly reduced the level of duty on many goods, making smuggling unprofitable. A much larger volume of goods then came in through the normal channels, making up for the reduction in duty, which in the case of tea was slashed from 127 per cent to a mere 12½ per cent.

One of the reasons why the local gentry connived with the Free Traders was the fact that the customs themselves were 'farmed' – sold to the highest bidder who undertook to pay a set annual sum to the government in return for the right to collect customs duty for himself. In this way the Government was sure of a guaranteed sum which it could immediately lay out in its estimates, while the 'farmers' could keep any profit they made on the deal. In this way the collection of Customs duty became something of a racket, and the local gentry felt perfectly justified in allying themselves with the smugglers to outwit these 'profiteers'.

As the ports were widely spaced round the coastline the tax farmers were localised, and there was no central organisation equipped to deal with the smuggling which rapidly increased to worrying proportions as far as the tax farmers were concerned. The Government, too, had cause for concern, as bids for the annual letting of the Customs were affected to great disadvantage by the leaks in the system represented by goods brought in out of sight of the Custom House. In 1729 it was reported that the Yarmouth Collector – the head of the Custom House there – estimated that, on the east coast alone, 17

All Saint's Church, Weston Longville, where Parson Woodforde was the vicar. Smuggling kept him and many of his contemporaries supplied with life's little luxuries.

an annual total of 180,000 gallons of brandy was being landed clandestinely. In 1734 another report stated that 54,000 pounds of tea and 123,000 gallons of brandy had been seized by the newly-formed patrols of Customs officers, and this, it was said, was but one-fifth of the total landed. It was appreciated that the Customs officers of the Revenue Service were demoralised by the well-organised, heavily-armed groups of smugglers who dared to bring large quantities of goods ashore in daylight.

The Revenue Service had its beginnings in 1698 when the illegal export of wool had reached such proportions that 299 'Riding Officers' were appointed by the Government to cover the coastal areas on horseback as a deterrent to the loading of wool or the landing of contraband on isolated coasts. By 1713 they were receiving support from garrisons of troops encamped at strategic points from which they could quickly give assistance to any place along the southern coast. As mounted infantrymen they were well equipped to challenge the smugglers' armed might.

Despite this the ensuing hundred years were the golden age of the smuggler. The Free Traders were probably better organised than the Revenue Service, and the odds were loaded in their favour: they could creep in by night at any one of a thousand landing places while the pathetically understaffed Revenue Service needed to keep the whole coast under surveillance. The Riding Officers were given an impossible job to do; they could not be in the saddle 24 hours a day, and they could not cover the whole area in daylight to check for signs of smuggling. The few successes they had, such as that of the fellow at Frinton who discovered a smuggler's hoard when the ground gave way beneath him, only proved how much was coming ashore undetected. Nevertheless despite the local feeling in favour of the smugglers – they were seen as local men doing daring deeds to bring in everyone's 'baccy and brandy at a cut price – there were plenty of applications for the Riding Officer's job. It had an official status under the protection of the law and though the salary was not all that grand the officer was awarded a share of every seizure of smuggler's cargo.

No doubt the presence of the Riding Officers was a deterrent to the fainter-hearted, but their comings and goings could be so easily monitored by the local community that their patrols were rendered ineffective. Their own employers, the Commissioners of Customs, did not place much confidence in this system of prevention, for the number of actual patrols undertaken by their Riding Officers could not be confirmed. They suspected that many of the journals which had to be entered up daily were fabrications, and even that, in some cases, the Riding Officer was hand-in-glove with the smuggler, earning a share of the proceeds simply by keeping out of the way on a dark night.

The sensible Riding Officer steered a middle course, pleasing his superiors with a well written-up journal, which showed how near he was to apprehending smugglers but for lack of sufficient support, and satisfying the community in which he had to live by hinting that a little quiet evasion of duty would go unnoticed if carried out in a tactful manner. The very real threat of retaliation by local people if one of their number was arrested and disappeared into the Navy was sufficient to cool the ardour of the keenest Riding Officer. (This punishment of being pressed into the Navy on the instant was very appropriate, for while it removed an experienced smuggler from the scene the Navy benefited from the man's seamanship.)

Another reason why the Riding Officer sometimes turned a blind eye was because he knew full well that many of the senior posts in the Customs service were filled by favour and nepotism rather than by selection for ability or experience. Geoffrey Morley puts it neatly in *Smuggling in Hampshire and Dorset 1700–1850*: 'Like many civil service posts of the 18th and early 19th century, the position of Customs Officer was a sinecure to be milked for whatever it could give.' But one can see from the reports that there were some men who did their best as Riding Officers, patrolling their allotted portion of coastline at irregular times of day and night to keep the smugglers guessing. A good horse was essential, and this they had to supply themselves, and pay for its upkeep, out of a salary of £42 per annum.

The sloops which had been introduced to catch the smugglers before the goods came ashore were also far from adequate to the task, as was shown by the first Parliamentary Enquiry into the extent of smuggling, made in 1736 under Sir John Cope, which concludes:

'The smugglers being grown to such a degree of violence, as to carry on the wicked practice by force and violence, not only in the country and the remote parts of the Kingdom, but even in the City of London itself going in gangs, armed with swords, pistols and . . . [other] weapons, even to the number of forty or fifty by which means they have been too strong not only for the officers of the Revenue but for the civil magistrates themselves . . . the sloops and boats appointed for preventing the running of goods have likewise frequently been beaten off by great numbers of armed men on board the smuggling vessels. The number of Custom House officers who have been beaten, abused and wounded since Christmas 1723, being no less than 250, besides six others who have actually been murdered in the execution of their duty.'

20   In response Parliament passed a new 'Indemnity for Smug-

glers' Act in 1736. The intention was that any smuggler who confessed and reported the names of his accomplices would be granted a free pardon. Meanwhile attacks on Revenue officers were to be punishable by death, and anybody who helped a smuggler by warning him off or assisting at a landing would be liable to one month's hard labour.

It is perhaps not surprising to learn that this Act was not very successful, for any man who informed on his smuggling comrades could be certain of death at *their* hands. In 1745 a Parliamentary Committee of Enquiry was told that in just six months the Suffolk coast alone had seen 1,835 horse-loads of tea and 1,689 such loads of spirits and other goods run ashore openly with armed guards of up to 70 men to convey them inland. It heard also that of the four million pounds of tea consumed each year in England only 800,000 pounds had passed through the Custom House and paid the appropriate duty. It was reckoned that as many as 30 landings were made every week around the coasts, and witnesses averred that the smugglers could make a profit if only one run in three was successful. The number of smugglers in organised gangs was put at 20,000.

Accordingly, an Act was introduced which made all smuggling activity at any level subject to the death penalty. To drum up support for the Revenue men, responsibility for smuggling activities not discovered and punished within six months was laid upon the county administration. A new ruse was built into the Act: since the smugglers were so hard to catch their names were to be published in the *London Gazette* or on 'Wanted' posters, informing them that they must surrender within 40 days or be subject to the instant imposition of the death penalty. Naturally enough, smugglers fought all the harder to evade capture.

In March 1783 a report was prepared by George Bishop, entitled *Observations, Remarks, and Means to Prevent Smuggling humbly submitted to the Consideration of the Rt. Honorable the House of Peers and the Honorable House of Commons, in Parliament assembled.* Though many of his statistics have since been questioned he does clearly describe the general situation at a time when smuggling was at its height, and we can believe him when he writes:

21

'The practice of smuggling has of late years made such rapid and gigantic strides from the sea coasts, into the very heart of the country, pervading every city, town and village, as to have brought universal distress upon the fair traders, from the most opulent and respectable, even to the smallest shopkeeper, and requires the united efforts of every honest man to aim at the suppression of it ... Smuggling is arrived to a height unprecedented in this or (perhaps) in any other nation in Europe; consequently the quantity and value of different articles thus illicitly imported must be immense; and, as they are paid for either in specie, or by smuggling of wool, which is worse, this traffic must greatly enrich the French, and other nations, and greatly impoverish this; and, while the fair traders are obliged to sustain various taxes to supply so great a deficiency in the revenue, they are deprived of their trade by a numerous banditti, who are become a terror to the King's officers, and a pest to the community; some hundreds of them having (frequently) been seen assembled together on horseback at one place, a sort of open rebellion highly inconsistent with, and greatly reproachful to, civil government.'

The range of goods taxed is shown, incidentally, by another point made in the report: 'I presume that smuggling is so much increased, the revenue will lose this year full three millions, which renders the taxes very unequal and more burthensome to the inland parts of the kingdom, as the inhabitants on the sea coast have their tea, spirits, wine, currants, raisins, starch, soap, china, glass and tobacco, mostly smuggled, they contribute nothing to the public purse for those articles, and of course all the inland counties must be taxed double in order to raise the taxes, which is a very great hardship.'

Bishop claims that in 1777 alone two and a half million gallons of geneva (gin) were smuggled into Britain from Dunkirk. 'Can there exist,' he concludes, 'an honest, considerate person in Great Britain, who upon perusing the case is not alarmed with the melancholy scene, and does not wish by all possible means to strike at the root of this infamous, pernicious traffic?'

William Goodwin of Earl Soham, halfway between Saxmundham and Stowmarket, kept a diary from 1785 to 1809 which has miraculously survived and come to the care of the Ipswich branch of the Suffolk Record Office. It is not so much a personal diary as a commonplace book reflecting his thoughts on all aspects of the life of the day. So taxation and its avoidance come in for comment:

'Jany. 1785. This young minister [Pitt] carried a Bill in the last Sessions for taking off the chief part of the duties on Teas & laying an addition on windows, call'd the Commutation Act, with a design to annihilate Smugling, whch. seems to answer its Intention – the Customs having increased £400,000 & the Excise a Million since ... previous to wh. the Contraband Trade sold two parts out of three of ye Teas consum'd in the Kingdom besides immense quantity of Spirits, insomuch that the Liquor & Tea Merchants totally declin'd Traveling for orders – It was a common thing almost daily to see Horses loaded with Tea & Carts with Spirits pass through this village unmolested; for almost all the People from the highest to the lowest were either directly or indirectly concern'd & of course abettors of the practice – private Gin & Tea shops were in every Parish to the great prejudice of the fair Trader & the morals of the common People: but now by operation of the Smugling Bill & the vigilance of the King's Cutters this shameful Business is nearly at an end, most of ye star-light Traders being ruin'd by the continual loss of their Cutters many of wh. are worth from five to thirty thousand Pounds.'

Having made these observations on the decline of smuggling Goodwin then rather contradicts himself with the record down to May of the smuggling activity he noticed in his village, which was some 15 miles from the coast at Sizewell:

'Feb. 1785. 2500 Gallons of smugled Spirits were carried thro' this village in 20 carts within the last six days.

'Feb 16. Five Smugling Carts past through this Village at 8 this morning loaded with 150 Tubs of Spirits containing 600 Gallons.'

He notes that though another five carts passed through a week later he had heard that 'The Soldiers' had been successful in seizing six such carts and their loads of spirits. They had another success on 2 March:

'15 Carts, 40 Horses & 600 Tubs of Spirits were seized this day at Sizewell by a party of Dragoons together with some Tea

An extract from William Goodwin's diary written in 1785. It mentions the reduction in tea duty which Prime Minister Pitt

& bale goods, notwithstanding which ye smuglers worked another cutter at ye same place the ensuing night.'

So Goodwin's record continues, until in April 1786 he tabulates very neatly a 'Calculation of Spirits Smuggled into Gt. Britain', wherein he reckons that, out of a total of 8,600,000 gallons imported by the smugglers, 1,500,000 came across the beaches of Essex, Suffolk and Norfolk.

The activity of Customs officers reached a peak in 1813, when the body of law and regulations in force on the subject was contained in no less than 2,100 Customs Acts – in all of which the smuggler seemed able to find a loophole.

Two years later the war with France was ended at Waterloo, and suddenly the Royal Navy had ships and men to spare to tackle the smuggling problem. The Revenue cutters were taken over by the Navy and, reinforced by the large, well-armed naval ships and the back-up of men and stores, they

24

thought would bring its smuggling to an end. (Reproduced by kind permission of The Suffolk Record Office)

turned from defensive to aggressive tactics. Very soon they had seized hundreds of thousands of gallons of brandy and gin, as many pounds of tea and tobacco, a host of other dutiable goods and no less than 875 ships confiscated from the smugglers. By 1817 a significant reduction in smuggling had been achieved which continued on down the years, receiving a great impetus in 1831 when the Coastguard Service was inaugurated.

It might be useful at this stage to summarise the legislation enacted throughout the period to deal with the smuggling problem since the Act of 1698 which attempted to check 'owling' by setting up the system of Riding Officers to patrol the coast. This Act also controlled dealing in wool within 15 miles of the coast.

1717 saw the introduction of a law which stated that smugglers who refused to plead could be sentenced to trans-

A spout lantern. Held in the crook of the left arm, the signaller's right hand covered the end of the spout, and was then removed to show a pin-point flash of light to an incoming boat.

portation. This was further strengthened by the Hovering Act of the following year which allowed small vessels – under 50 tons – to be seized if they were observed to be loitering within six miles of the coast; such vessels would be automatically seized if on examination they were found to be carrying dutiable goods.

In 1721 another Smuggling Act introduced a sentence of up to seven years' transportation upon conviction for smuggling. A limitation on the number of oars used to propel any particular boat was also introduced on a regional basis; in the south no more than four oars were allowed. Tea was added to the list of dutiable goods in 1724, and bonded warehouses were introduced to facilitate the proper regulation of imports and the payment of duty on a wide class of goods.

After a Parliamentary Inquiry in 1736 under the chairmanship of Sir John Cope another Smuggling Act was passed. This increased the penalties, particularly for armed assault on

Revenue officers. Even if unarmed, any smuggler resisting arrest could, on conviction, be transported to the colonies – from whence the chance of return was very faint indeed.

The duty on tea was cut in 1745, following a Parliamentary Inquiry into that trade, yet it was found necessary to increase penalties against those intended smugglers found loitering within six miles of the coast. A year later, in response to a steady increase in smuggling, a new Act brought in the most severe punishment so far. Offenders risked the death penalty, not only for landing contraband or joining a band of men in an attempt to do so, but also for merely harbouring a smuggler. Those smugglers who, in armed resistance, killed a Government man would be hanged on the gibbet at the place of their crime. Where the perpetrator of the murder or injury of an officer could not be established the county as a whole would be charged £100 for such a murder and £40 for an injury. The Act also arranged that the names of known smugglers would be published in the *London Gazette*. Such men were to surrender to their trial within 40 days of the announcement or they would be judged guilty in their absence and the appropriate sentence would be pronounced in advance of their apprehension. For any informer who cared to take the great personal risk of identifying and bringing to book these named smugglers there was a reward of £500.

In the next 15 years further legislation increased the duty on tea and controlled more closely the trade in gin and tobacco. Then after a period of increasing laxity in the observation of the law the 1779 Act was passed, re-defining both the crime and its punishment; extending the limitation on the number of oars to a boat to four only in all regions; and establishing severe penalties for gaolers who allowed smugglers to escape, before or after trial. Three years later the Act of Oblivion of 1782 allowed smugglers a pardon for their crimes on a sliding scale, according to the number of men they could bring forward to serve in the armed forces. If a convicted smuggler could find two soldiers and two sailors to serve His Majesty, then he could go scot free.

In 1783 the Commission of Excise reported on the problems involved in counteracting smuggling. As a result, in the following year William Pitt the Younger, then Prime Minister, cut

A Smuggler and *The Preventive Service*, two prints of the 1830s, which illustrate the clothes of the smuggler and the uniform and equipment of a Coastguard.

the duty on tea by a staggering 114½ per cent to bring it down to just 12½ per cent, thus taking it off the smuggler's shopping list of profitable contraband. He recouped some of the lost revenue (much of which was already lost through smuggling) by introducing the famous Window Tax, the effect of which can be seen even today in the facades of many older houses where the windows were bricked in to avoid paying the tax.

28   The Customs had good information on the way in which

boats were specially built to suit the smugglers, so at the same time regulations were introduced defining very strict limits of construction in an effort to discourage the practice.

Further control was established when the Preventive Waterguard was formed from 1809 under the aegis of the Customs, though in 1816 it passed to independent status under a Comptroller-General. It was in that year that the Revenue cutters were placed under the control of the Admiralty.

In 1817 the authorities adopted another strategy in the south-east of the country, called the Coast Blockade. This established look-out points actually within sight and signal of each other, and covered the coast from Sheerness round to Seaford. On other coasts the Coast Blockade was rendered unnecessary by the introduction of the Coastguard, one of the reforms put forward by the Commission of 1822 which observed: 'We do not find that any concert has been practically established between the several authorities, nor does it appear that any communications exist between the executive officers in the different services . . .' It went on to say that the reforms it suggested would introduce a uniform system of control by one responsible authority: 'In this system the primary force will be that which is now called the Preventive Water Guard, although from the change in the nature of its duties since its first establishment the term "Coast Guard" would be a more appropriate distinction.' It was not until 1831 that the Coastguard replaced the Coast Blockade in the south-east.

The Coastguard was a civilian service run by the Customs in the same way as it had run the Preventive Water Guard. It was taken over by the Admiralty in 1831 but continued on the same basis until, in 1845, it was absorbed into the Naval Reserve. When the Coastguard was introduced one of the conditions of employment was that boatmen must be stationed 20 miles or more from their homes: a reflection of the common problem of collusion arising as a result of local pressure on, and even blackmail of Revenue men in their own communities.

By the time the men were numbered on the strength of the Naval Reserve the integrated service introduced in 1822 had proved more than a match for the professional smuggler, and the removal of duty from a wide range of goods by Prime Minister Peel in 1845 meant that a man could not make a living worth all the risks involved.

2

The Impact on East Anglia

The coastline of Essex is formed largely of very thick and solid London clay which can be seen as cliffs to the north at Walton on the Naze and to the south at Southend-on-Sea where it affects the colour of the sand in the estuarine shallows. Overlying the clay are extensive glacial drift deposits, and the gravel eroded from these is the basis of beaches from the Thames to the Wash. The chalk which forms the pleasant hills of northwest Essex beyond Saffron Walden makes that area essentially a corn-growing countryside, and at Thurrock it was extensively quarried in the 18th century for whiting and lime, and also for the basic chalk itself which was taken by barge round the coast and up the creeks and rivers to be spread on the fields to improve fertility.

On the clay in the north of Essex cereals grew well, and in the centre mixed farming was profitable. The gentle hills in the south and the fertile grazing lands of the marshes behind the shoreline supported vast flocks of sheep from medieval times – though the flocks decreased as the centre of the cloth trade moved north – and a feature which has been described as 'the market-gardening plain', a belt of good-hearted land three to five miles wide, reached out from London north of the Thames to the coast.

Employment for the majority of people in Essex was on the farm, on the sea in the fishing fleets or as domestic servants in other people's houses.

In the 18th century farmwork was extremely badly paid, and to an agricultural labourer the attraction of easy money for a night's work assisting the smugglers was almost irresistible. Since farming was a major industry in Essex, the smugglers could rely on a large pool of sympathisers and helpers in the county.

As to fishing, it should be remembered that Barking, then a busy Essex port on the Thames, had the largest fishing fleet in the world. The 'Short Blue Fleet' built up by Samuel Hewett in the last quarter of the 18th century numbered around 220 smacks at the height of its operations in 1850. Crewing these boats nurtured the skills of seamanship so essential to the smugglers' trade.

Many adults and children were employed in the 'big houses' from which merchants, investors, politicians and professional people commuted to the capital, using the same highways down which the contraband travelled to a rich and eager market. These servants were often useful as go-betweens who could arrange deals between their employers, the consumers, and their relatives who were involved in the smuggling.

The rivers of the three counties are prominent features of the landscape, and they were very useful to the smuggler. Essex alone has 22 separately identified rivers. The erosion of the whole coast forms sandbanks; these encourage the deposition of river silt in deltas which form winding creeks behind offshore, sandbanked shallows, providing innumerable labyrinthine escape routes for smugglers on the run.

Suffolk is a smaller county divided from Essex to the south by the Stour and from Norfolk to the north by the Waveney. Here the important geological formation is the stony Suffolk Crag which, with the remains of glacial deposits, forms the low cliffs of easily eroded sand, gravel, and clay. Despite the high rate of erosion there are many coastal features which formed landmarks for sailors and smugglers alike: the long shingle spit of Orford Ness; the stretches of little sandy hillocks called denes; the wide estuaries of the Stour, Deben and the Orwell; and the Oulton and Fritton Decoy broads between the Waveney and the sea, where the river turns sharply and flows north towards Great Yarmouth.

As in Essex, those who did not serve the gentry or fish the North Sea were locked in labour on the land. There were, of course, all the usual crafts and industries characteristic of local self-sufficiency in the 18th century – from brickmaking in the brick-earth deposits to the fashioning of gun flints from the flint beds at Brandon. Boat building and repair was an industry taken for granted all along the coast, and the craftsmen showed their art in the lively boats commissioned by the smugglers to outsmart the fastest Revenue cutter. The 'fossilised' wool town of Lavenham with its church built by rich wool merchants is a reminder that the weavers here needed an endless supply of fleeces, and the shepherd was an important link in the chain. In the case of wool, smuggling occurred in the reverse direction; the much-admired wool and the cloth itself found a very ready sale on the Continent which the smugglers exploited to the full.

The skull-like shape of the county of Norfolk juts out determinedly into the North Sea. There are comparatively high cliffs at Hunstanton and in the Cromer area, and low cliffs between Mundesley and Yarmouth; salt-marshes between Hunstanton and Sheringham; low, marshy land in the Fens on the west; and the Broads in the east. The county has a very long coastline, facing a sea with a bad reputation. It has a great tradition of sailors, one of the most famous being Horatio Nelson. At the height of the smuggling story he was fighting the French and clearing them from the seas around the world. At the same time smugglers were risking their lives in more secretive fashion, running the gauntlet of the Government and the enemy to make a fortune out of contraband brought across the Channel in small sailing boats under the very noses of the combatants.

In those days the Essex coast was found to be particularly suitable for the sinking of contraband which could be recovered later. The Revenue men could be outwitted more easily in this fashion, for the smugglers could weight their contraband, drop it overboard, mark the spot by a landmark or an insignificant buoy, and then hide among the oyster-dredgers busy about their lawful occupation in the creeks and estuaries. The Crouch, the Roach and the Blackwater all offered excellent opportunities for this type of smuggling until the introduction of the Preventive Water Guard in 1809 under the aegis of the Customs authority. Until that time, Essex men made a good living without risking the physical battles of the early days.

This trick of hiding among the oyster dredgers clearly

33

Smugglers, a print of 1799 engraved by J. P. Smith, which shows the typical features of a small landing. (Reproduced by kind permission of Alan Hay)

demonstrates the size of the oyster industry in East Anglian waters. The situation was unusual. While all the organised oyster fisheries exported to the Netherlands, the Crouch and Leigh fisheries catered for such a large demand that they also imported oysters from the Channel Islands. At that time the oyster was food for the common man as well as the Lord of the Manor. In the first quarter of the 19th century oyster-layings were centred on the Colne, the Blackwater, the Crouch, the Roach and off Leigh-on-Sea in the Thames estuary.

The duty on exported oysters was abolished in 1812, but there were many other opportunities for smuggling. Having unloaded their oysters, the dredgers were often tempted to bring back a little something from the Continent. Dutch vessels involved in the oyster trade also tried to make a little extra from spirits and tobacco brought in as they came to collect their oysters. During the winter thousands of bushels of oysters were imported from Jersey in boats operating out of Maldon. As Hervey Benham says in *The Smugglers' Century* 'Needless to say the Customs were interested in more than oysters when the Jersey smacks came in.'

The coast of Suffolk and Norfolk is more clearly defined than the coast of Essex, meeting the sea in low cliffs with good landing places in the gaps where streams have worn gentle valleys. These were easily scaled by pack-horses loaded pannier-style with tubs of brandy and sacks of a hundred-and-one attractive items made luxuries by the tax imposed upon them. Accordingly the smugglers here were more plentiful and better organised than their Essex counterparts.

The men who had the greatest opportunity to smuggle whilst going about their everyday business were the crews of the packet boats which provided the link with the Continent via ports like Harwich. They carried the mail and sailed as regularly as the weather permitted. The packet boats were owned by their captains who contracted to carry the mails for the Post Office. One of the terms of the agreement was that the crew must be no less than eight including the master. In practice the master usually found it necessary to employ extra crew if the ship was to be worked effectively.

The sailors were paid less than six shillings a week, although their food was provided while they were on board.

When the ferry could not put out, the crew had to go ashore and find their own food. In such hard times the temptation to earn some easy money by smuggling a little contraband was too powerful to resist. These packet boats were much bigger than the Revenue cutters which frequently stopped them at sea to search them. Much friction and hostility was engendered as the Revenue men were keen to earn shares in the value of any seizure while the packet crews were, naturally, equally concerned that the goods on which they had spent their miserable wages should not be found and confiscated. Not only that, many a man who was caught in the act of smuggling was immediately pressed into the Navy. Paradoxically these east coast seamen were so experienced in braving the vagaries of the Channel and the North Sea that they were welcomed into the Royal Navy and often gained rapid promotion. To the rough crews of the great ships of the line they were heroes, for they had challenged authority, defied the Revenue men and showed a great spirit of adventure and comradeship in their daring dark-night runs.

Fred Roe, writing his *Essex Survivals* some 60 years ago, reckoned that the coast of Essex and, by implication, that of Norfolk and Suffolk too, presented 'an agreeable opportunity for the exercise of ingenuity in the matter of smuggling'. Two hundred years before him Daniel Defoe contended that the one main industry from Essex to Land's End was smuggling. It has been said that smugglers around the East Anglian coast made a good profit even if only one in four of their runs was successful. The local people engaged in auxiliary capacities by the smugglers were the losers, for when they were employed on an operation which failed, they got nothing.

The smuggling baron who led his gang from the front would not have stayed in the business unless he was making a handsome profit. One such gang leader was a man named Hunwick, of whom an unusual memorial can still be seen in the Colchester and Essex Museum. It is a set of hydrometers which he bought from a Mr Thurston of St Botolph's Street in Colchester. He would have used them to check the strength of the spirits he was illegally importing in very large quantities. The Schiedam and other distilleries just across the water were set up to answer the demand from the East Anglian smugglers.

Smugglers Attacked. A popular early 19th century print by an unknown artist. (Reproduced by kind permission of Alan Hay)

Hunwick was successful for a long time, probably because of his own inspiring leadership and his attention to detail, but there came the day when his luck ran out. He was conducting a convoy of wagons inland when one of them broke down in the lane leading from Dedham Lock. The Revenue men pounced, and Hunwick languished for six very uncomfortable months in Chelmsford Gaol.

The action when smugglers were caught red-handed could be very hot, for the smugglers not only had an unpleasant time ahead of them if they were apprehended, but they also lost their share of a very profitable enterprise which made their fisherman's or labourer's wages look very small beer. A Revenue man's pocket pistol, popularly known then as a 'barker', which was found in the soil under a hedge at Thundersley and is now to be seen in the museum at Colchester, conjures up a picture of just such a desperate fight, a terrible injury, and the loss of the pistol in the mêlée.

Such an incident would have been reported by word of mouth in the surrounding villages until it became a vague rumour, spreading wider and wider like the ripples from a stone thrown in the village pond. In all three counties the seaside villages were remote, and newspapers were read only by a small educated minority. The smuggling exploits were arranged verbally, and lowered voices spread the news of landings in the locality. Folk who lived more than a mere five miles away would be looked on as foreigners.

The attraction of the cash paid to the local men and boys for acting as look-outs, landing guides, members of beach parties or horsemen was summed up by the local poet George Crabbe, writing at the time it was all happening. In *The Village*, published in 1783 after revision by Edmund Burke and Dr Samuel Johnson, Crabbe countered the current craze for a romantic, idealised picture of rural life with a down-to-earth account of harshness and hardship in the remoteness of the Suffolk countryside. He writes of the plight of the young men of his native village, Aldeburgh:

Where are the swains, who, daily labour done,
With rural games play'd down the setting sun;
Where now are these? – Beneath yon cliff they stand,
To show the freighted pinnace where to land;
To load the ready steed with guilty haste,
To fly in terror o'er the pathless waste,
Or, when detected, in their straggling course,
To foil their foes by cunning or by force:
Or yielding part (which equal knaves demand),
To gain a lawless passport through the land.

39

The impact of smuggling on daily life even well inland can be fully appreciated from a single sheet written out by a man, presumably a constable, as his report on a complicated case of smuggling on 20 September 1678 at Ilford in Essex, heading it *The Information of George Best.*

Two troopers billetted locally came to Best and asked him if he had the power to seize uncustomed or prohibited goods. On hearing his affirmative the troopers said they could tell him where 'a parcell of them were and desired him to goe along with them immediately which they did; and goinge towards Ilford G— B— desired to know the person of ye Suspicion. They told him they had quartered about a month at ye rose and crown in Greate Ilford and had observed that in that time a Coache which they supposed came from Ipswich called there twice before this time and had delivered each time a sacke which was tyed behind the Coach to Williams his wife that kept the alehouse tellinge her there was a toaken for her which she receeved and about the same time that ye Coache came there was a gentleman or two with an empty portmanteau which they filled with things out of the sacke & likewise their trowsers & in the duske of the evening rode towards London.

'The day being Wednesday the 28 August last they observinge ye Coachman to deliver a sacke to Williams his wife as Formerly and Mr. Rolfeson and Langly merchants, G— B— was informed, were at the same alehouse.' Then the troopers and George Best 'proceedinge towards the alehouse met these two merchants within a mile of Ilford, the trooper knowinge of them tooke hould of there bridles and immediately G— B— layed his hand upon ye portmanteau und declared that he ceased [seized] all prohibited goods within the portmanteau and what they likewise had about them that were prohibited: for ye use of ye King's upon which one of them Mr. Rolphson as was supposed delivered out of his trowsers 11 parcels which appeared to be narrow prohibited rebins [ribbons].

'The Troopers havinge gotten ye portmanteau, refused to go with G— B— to Bow where he intended to secure the portmanteau and ye other goods for ye Kings use but would returne to William his house at Ilford. G— B— went there with them the two merchants goeing alonge with them, G— B— desired ye troopers to take care & to secure Mr. Langly

Drawing showing the sort of underwear used for smuggling lace, as found on smugglers captured by the authorities. (Reproduced by kind permission of H.M. Commissioners of Customs and Excise)

that he might have an accompte [account] what goods he had about him, wich they promised they would doe, but when G— B— enquired for him they sayd he was gone. Then G— B— enquired for the portmanteau . . .' One of the troopers assured Best that the portmanteau was safely locked up in his room at the inn, but Best reports that he never did see it again, and we are to see why: 'One of ye troopers tould G— B— that ye woman of ye house had some goods in her aperull [apparell] and upon examining it she had six parcels of narrow prohibited ribbon which G— B— ceased [seized] and layd them to ye 11 parcels that were found about Mr. Rolfeson.'

Then one of the crafty troopers said he would look after the 17 parcels 'and deliver them the next morninge to ye Commissioners of ye Customes & trust to them for a reward for the extraordinary paines that he had taken'. When George Best asked after the soldiers the next morning they had gone, but luckily he found them quite by chance at an alehouse in Little Ilford. He was a brave man – he demanded the portmanteau and the other goods from them. The trooper coolly replied 'that ye Merchants had treated them very civilly & rewarded them with money very nobelly to the contente of him seelfe

41

Eighteen Rows in the above Waistcoat or Stays, well stuff'd with Tea, weighing about 8 lbs.

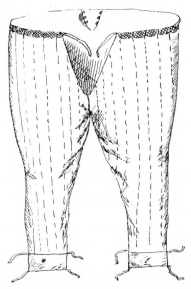

The above worn is a pair of drawers, made of Stout Cotton, secured with strong drawing Strings, stuff'd with Tea, and weighing about 16 lbs.

Waistcoat and drawers made of stout cotton were stuffed with tea by carriers of contraband. (Reproduced by kind permission of H.M. Commissioners of Customs and Excise)

and his comrades, upon which they had delivered the portmanteau and the other parcels to ye Merchants the last night'.
The ease of smuggling, the way it pervaded the community,
and its acceptance by rich and poor alike is amply demonstrated.

The general attitude of the people among whom the smugglers moved with such confidence and such freedom is summed up well by J. M. Scott in *The Tea Story*: 'This general
sympathy for the free traders was the most important factor in
the struggle. Not only would nobody inform against them, but
farms with their barns and haystacks, even churches with their
crypts and tombs made excellent caches. Tea and tobacco
were such harmless things. As for brandy, if the Government
had to have taxes why couldn't they tax something else?'

The impact of increasing duty on tea is shown very clearly
by comparing the price of 10s.6d. a pound which Parson
Woodforde paid smuggler Andrews for tea in 1777, and the
price of 16s.0d. a pound which the good widow Minter found
she had to charge in her Ipswich shop in 1764 for 'legitimate'
tea. It was not until 1784 that Pitt the Younger reduced the
tax on tea from 127 per cent to 12½ per cent, and the bottom
fell out of the tea smugglers' market.

Another man of the cloth who helped lend respectability to
the doubtful 'free trade' was the Rector of Great Bealings,
Suffolk, from 1804 to 1837. The Reverend Philip Meadows
lived in his rectory on the bank of Martlesham Creek where
the Deben broadens into an estuary. He had a very useful
pony and chaise, and he left his stable door unlocked on
moonless nights. That well-known chaise guaranteed free
passage past enquiring excisemen and curious village constables. The smugglers coming up the creek were grateful for
this heaven-sent opportunity to get their contraband well
away so quickly. The Rector may or may not have heard the
creaking of the stable door, but he only had to poke about in
his shrubbery: if he came across a keg which gurgled pleas-
antly he knew his pony and chaise had been borrowed.

Places associated with smuggling in South Essex.

3

From the Thames to the Blackwater

London's river washes nearly 40 miles of the Essex boundary. In the 18th century the Thames was a highway which enabled goods to be distributed over a wide area of southern England. To the Londoners of the day it was as convenient, and as taken for granted, as a motorway is today. The capital dealt with more than two-thirds of the country's foreign trade – and most of it came in by water up the Thames. The series of Navigation Acts introduced by Cromwell in 1651 to stem the Dutch trade with the English colonies, and strengthened early in the 18th century, laid down that certain goods including tobacco and sugar had to be routed via London whatever their destination.

With thousands of tons of goods going up the estuary in sailing ships, boats and barges, there were many opportunities for off-loading and transferring contraband. London was the most densely populated city in Britain, housing some 675,000 people, and it offered a good market for the go-between dealer. He would arrange for smuggled goods to arrive at his storehouse after dark, then in no time at all they were moved on via a distributive network. Hundreds of minor dealers swarmed about the big merchant ships and Naval vessels back from foreign parts, looking for bargains in contraband. From the docks at Gravesend, boats laden with such booty could easily be rowed across the river to the Essex bank. In 1724 Daniel Defoe reckoned he could count up to 2,000 ships loading and unloading in the Pool of London, and in that noisy chaos there were a hundred and one opportunities to slip contraband overboard into the bumboats which plied their trade as provision merchants to the ships, or onto the quays and into the carts specially hired to get the stuff away quickly.

Tilbury Fort and the Thames with the ferry in the foreground, from a print by Campion in 1830.

At Gravesend, as tide and weather permitted, a Customs officer was taken on board each ship to check on cargo and crew for contraband as it proceeded upstream to the Pool of London. This one man, living on a ship for several days entirely at the mercy of a crew who had brought their contraband thousands of miles to bolster their miserable pay, was not going to risk his life by looking in odd corners for a plug of tobacco. The larger ships, like the East Indiamen with their deep draught, had to stop at Deptford and tranship their cargoes to boats and barges. Other ships littered the river from there on upwards as they waited in a long untidy queue for their turn to put in at a quay. In the confusion of these movements and manoeuvres were endless opportunities for smuggling ashore not just personal contraband but also quantities of the actual cargo.

So Essex men on Thames-side could bring their carts to the waterside and push out in their little boats to see what they could pick up: the returns were more than worth the risk. Tea, for example, could be bought in Europe for two shillings (ten pence) a pound, but duty on tea in England brought the price up to five shillings (twenty-five pence) a pound. This was in

46

the middle of the 18th century when 90 per cent of English adults drank tea, and half that tea had been smuggled to evade the tax. The river Thames was a broad highway to the smugglers' Eldorado.

From Shoeburyness, at the very limit of the estuary, ships made their way past Prittlewell and its South End, which was then but a fishing hamlet, to Leigh. This was an old port which was already silting up in the 18th century. It still had enough water to allow small trading schooners access, and they could hide in amongst the local oyster dredgers and make well-organised transfers of contraband. A Custom House was established here early on.

In his progress up the Thames, the sailor had to beware of low-lying Canvey Island, which was one of a number of large shifting sandbanks until it was permanently salvaged from the tidal Thames by Vermuyden's Dutch drainage experts in 1625. The island lies off South Benfleet and Hadleigh Marsh, and was separated from the mainland by Benfleet Creek and Hadleigh Ray where, even then, the great castle on the hill was a crumbling ruin. Further up the estuary lay the Essex Marshes: from Corringham through Stanford-le-Hope, Mucking, Tilbury, and right up to Hornchurch and Barking Creek, they gave endless opportunities for bringing goods ashore where only locals knew the winding ways through tide-washed mud-flats.

In the late 18th century Barking had a flourishing fishing fleet. Samuel, son of Scrymgeour Hewett, had introduced the principle of refrigeration to get the fish back to port as fresh as possible. Using a single ship loaded with ice from the big Barking icehouse, the fish was collected and rushed back to port while a hundred or more trawlers of his Short Blue Fleet stayed on their fishing stations.

The fishermen Hewett employed led a very hard life for little pay. If they could come alongside a ship outside territorial waters and take on a few items of contraband they could make a tidy profit, providing they could get the goods ashore undetected. 'Coopering', as this system was called, was widely practised. Barking Creek ran on up to Ilford, and from there it was but a step down the High Road to the City of London and the folk with money to pay for such smuggled luxuries.

47

At this time the Essex coast from the Thames to the Blackwater was remote and inaccessible, indented with creeks, periodically flooded by the tide and beset by mudflats and sandbanks. Frank Martin, in his *Rogues' River*, writes 'The Essex shore was more tricky because of the large expanse of the Maplin Sands. Those who knew the area could use the tide to slip into Havengore Channel on the flood and get into the Roach, where places like Paglesham, Great Stambridge and Rochford were good smugglers' haunts.'

The river Roach loops and winds through many creeks to make a multitude of islands, and all suffer from repeated inundation. Havengore, Potton, Foulness and Wallasea islands are the largest of these. The Roach joins the Crouch as it runs out to sea along the north edge of Foulness Island; just a little upstream stands Burnham-on-Crouch, an old port and modern yachting mecca. More than 15 miles inland, almost up to Hullbridge and the new town of South Woodham Ferrers, there is an indentation in the course of the Crouch which is still known as Brandy Hole, in reference to the smuggling trade.

North of Burnham, behind what was in those days an inadequate sea wall, the marshes stretched north through Southminster, Dengie, Tillingham and Bradwell to the bank of the Blackwater. Up its estuary Osea and Northey Islands make the approach to Maldon a wild and winding waterway. This stretch of Essex coast from Thames to Blackwater offered a huge variety of smuggling opportunities. Such was the smuggling of contraband all along this coast that the Government, alarmed at the loss of revenue, introduced special sloops to cruise offshore and up the estuaries in an attempt to prevent the illicit trade. One ship was on station as early as 1695 and another was introduced three years later. Two ships were not enough to have any effect as a deterrent and the trade continued, to the extent that in 1707 even the soldiers in the garrison of Tilbury Fort were accused of being involved in smuggling ventures.

Dick Turpin, the notorious highwayman born at Hempstead in 1705, mixed his highway robbery business with smuggling forays. He allied himself with the Gregory Gang, hiding the contraband in the cellars of the ruined Hadleigh

A pottery 'fairing' of Dick Turpin. Born at Hempstead in Essex, he became a notorious highwayman and smuggler.

Castle until it could safely be sent on through the Essex hinterland. In February 1735 the *General Evening Post* reported that a member of this gang had been accused of smuggling, and in a letter of 14 December 1736 the correspondent wrote of the same gang whose crimes included smuggling and deer stealing. Turpin added another dimension to the art; if he knew the habits of a smuggler, and when he would be travelling with the profits of his illegal activity, Turpin was quite capable of lying in wait for him and taking his money at the point of a pistol.

Further confirmation of considerable smuggling activity in this area is to be found in Daniel Defoe's description of Faversham, Kent in 1726: 'As to the landing of goods here from Holland and France, such as wine and brandy from the latter, and pepper, tea, coffee, callicoes, tobacco and such goods ... that black trade has not only been carry'd on here, as I was informed, but on both sides of the river [the Thames] on the Essex as well as the Kentish shores.'

The *Chelmsford Chronicle* of 10 October, 1764 shows how the tax on the 'callicoes' Defoe mentions, and on many other kinds of material encouraged smuggling: 'Lately was seized and brought to the Custom-house at Leigh, Essex, (by Mr. Thomas Lee, Surveyor of that place) several thousand ells of French blond-lace, brocades and flower'd silks; a quantity of womens leather gloves; ditto muslin-ruffles and aprons, wrought with threads, cambricks and lawns; Tapestry, silk-stockings, gimp, pearl-beads, chrystal-stones, and watch-chains, some gold tissue shapes for waistcoats, brocaded with gold and silk; also a quantity of book-muslin and East-India goods.'

Leigh Custom House was kept busy in the receipt and storage of seized cargoes of contraband goods. In 1768 a smuggler's sloop stopped off Maldon was sailed round to Leigh where its haul of gin, brandy, tea, muslin and other attractively untaxed items was taken into the Custom House before the boat itself was burnt as a warning to other aspiring smugglers. A sale there in 1781 of boats and contraband seized from smugglers included 680 gallons of geneva (gin), 82 of brandy, 47 of rum, 275 quarters of port, 28 of 'lisbon', 120 of claret, 33 yards of calico, 'much foreign china', together with a sloop and a smaller sailing boat. Around 1786 John Loten,

The foreshore at Leigh in 1830. The Custom House overlooked the boats which sailed in and out of the port.

Collector of Customs at Leigh, reported that he knew of at least ten local boats which were engaged in smuggling. Some of these boats were owned by two families related by marriage, the Dowsetts and the Blyths of Leigh and Paglesham.

William Dowsett had a cutter called the *Neptune*, armed with six swivel guns and sailed by a crew of 11. One November day in 1778, on the French coast, it took on two ankers and 391 half-ankers of brandy, rum and gin. Since an anker was a barrel holding roughly 8½ imperial gallons, the smugglers loaded a total of more than 1600 gallons of spirits into their vessel. To that they added three hundredweight of tobacco, two hundredweight of coffee and eight hundredweight of tea. Creeping cautiously through the Whitaker Channel off the Crouch estuary at sunrise they were spotted by a look-out in the Revenue cutter *Bee*, which was riding at anchor close inshore.

The *Bee* quickly got under way, chased the smuggler and drew level with it, calling on the crew to heave-to and submit to a search. During an hour-long confrontation Dowsett and his crew cursed and reviled the Revenue men, while refusing

51

to heave-to and trying to pull away. Captain Hart of the *Bee* ordered a shot to be fired across their bows, but this only brought a volley from the swivel guns of the *Neptune*. Fire was returned from the *Bee* and two of the ringleaders, William Riches and James Anderson, were killed; without them the crew quickly gave up.

John Dowsett, whose exact relationship to William cannot now be established, was master of another ship working out of Leigh, taking legitimate cargoes across the Channel. Business was good enough, but the temptation to return with contraband and make money twice over was too great to resist. Dowsett's boat *Big Jane* was well-armed with at least half-a-dozen six-pounder brass cannon, but they were to no avail against the Revenue men; a report from Harwich dated 31 May 1780, printed in the *Essex Chronicle*, states: 'A large lugsail boat commanded by — Dowsett, a notorious smuggler, was brought in this afternoon by the Argus cutter, capt. Haggis, and the Bee cutter, capt. Hart: she was taken this morning on the Essex coast by a boat from each cutter, well manned and armed, after a chase of 11 hours, and a smart firing on both sides, in which the lugger had three men wounded, and her hull and sails damaged; the cutter's people received no hurt: their prize's cargo consists of 23 cwt. of tea, and 252 half ankers of Geneva, brandy and rum; the smugglers made their escape by taking to their small boat.'

In these sandbank-strewn waters a rowing boat could cross shallows where a cutter could not hope to follow. Another report in the same column shows how busy the Revenue cutters were: 'Thursday last arrived the Argus cutter, C[apt]. Haggis, with 100 half ankers of Geneva; and sailed again on a cruise.'

In 1783 the Maldon Collector of Customs complained that smugglers were taking on such large crews that the Revenue officers did not care to apprehend them. One such boat he mentioned as 'a cutter supposed to belong to Wm. Dowsett at Paglesham, which carries ten men'.

William Blyth, an oyster merchant who lived at Paglesham and died there in 1830 aged 74, was William Dowsett's son-in-law. When he bought a boat, the *Tartar* in 1794, he was described as an oyster dredger.

Dowsett and Blyth worked together in a smuggling gang which included men named Emberson and Brown. They are remembered in the autobiography of John Harriott, himself a colourful character, who lived on Rushley Island in the 1780s. He was the originator of the Thames River Police in 1800, so he knew all the criminal element associated with smuggling. On one occasion when he needed a passage home from France he sought for Blyth's boat at Dunkirk, because he knew that Blyth would land in Essex just a mile and a half from his home. But on visiting the tavern which Blyth haunted he found only Kentish men. They invited him to eat with them while they waited for the Essex gang. In the alcoholic aftermath someone proposed a toast: 'Damnation to all Revenue laws and officers.' Harriott told them they were proposing the wrong toast, for if the laws were abolished that would mean the end of smuggling – and of their livelihood. The smugglers saw the sense of that and turned the toast around to 'Revenue laws and officers for ever.' In due course Blyth arrived, and Harriott was carried off as a kind of trophy in celebration of Essex wit triumphing over the men from Kent.

While editing selections from the records of the Customs Outport of Maldon in 1923, the librarian of H.M. Customs and Excise wrote: 'There is no doubt that a very great deal of smuggling at one time took place along this coast yet the records do not seem to show that the officers were very successful in dealing with it, the seizures being comparatively few. In fact those low-lying lands with winding creeks full of dangerous shoals and mud-banks would probably be a playground for the expert smuggler with a thorough local knowledge of his ground in the days when lights and buoys and printed sailing directions were non-existent.'

It does appear from the communications sent out by the Board of Commissioners in London that they felt it necessary to keep reminding the Maldon Collector of the need for continual vigilance. In August 1744, having heard that seven East Indiamen had arrived in the Downs under a convoy of two men-of-war, they wagged their corporate finger, 'it being apprehended that great quantities of goods will be attempted to be run from the said ships . . . be very careful in looking out [to prevent such efforts]'.

Bow Bridge drawn by W. Bartlett about 1830. This bridge crossed the river Lea on the smugglers' high road to London and their profitable markets.

In 1749 a further adjuration was issued, for the Board had 'received information that there is now lading at Rotterdam with tea, muslins, etc., a black cutter. She has two new cloths in the after part of her mainsail and it is reported she will land her cargo on your coast'. Diligence was demanded in keeping a look-out for this vessel. The Board knew this part of the coast was not yet effectively patrolled, and in July 1763 they were able to introduce the cutter *Hector*, sailed by a naval crew under Lieutenant Charles Garencies. She cannot have called in at Maldon very often, for John Leather in *The Salty Shore* maintains that 'Until 1775 the Blackwater smugglers had an easy time as the yawl *Queen* was the river's sole anti-smuggling vessel and was kept at Maldon for the use of Thomas Sherman, the "Tide Surveyor". She was easily spotted whenever she slipped down on the ebb and Sherman complained bitterly of lack of support from his masters.' It has to be said that Lieutenant Garencies had an almost impossible task in that he was directed 'to cruise from Harwich along the coast of Essex to Sheerness to prevent the infamous practice of smuggling'.

54

There was always the problem of infiltration of the service by smugglers' 'moles'. Smugglers living locally could put tremendous pressure on Customs men who lived cheek by jowl with them. This is illustrated by the case of humble William Rowlings, boatman at Mersea Island who, said the Collector in 1733, 'is suspected to keep a correspondence with the smugglers'. The loyalty of such boatmen was at times severely tested. Look at the experience of Christopher Francis and Nicholas Billbo, boatmen at Burnham who, on 25 June 1767, took their boat out to Wallasea Island and seized a small craft with contraband on board. Then, 'seeing a small Dover boat who came to an anchor they then proceeded to row up to her in order to have boarded her but before they could get up to her they hoisted up their sail and came by the said Francis and Billbo . . . the master George Foxell . . . swore if they offered to come on board they would knock them down and held up the handspikes for that purpose . . . Francis and Billbo do verily believe that they had some smuggled goods on board . . . George Foxell is a dredgerman and lives in the parish of Paglesham'.

Though the Collector reported in November 1783 that he knew of no increase in smuggling in the Maldon area over the previous three years, he went on to write that the smugglers' tactics had been 'to carry a greater number of hands in their cutters than our officers dare attack and when they land their goods will guard them by night to their destined places to lodge them and bid defiance to any officers who dare oppose'. He followed this with a list of ships believed to be employed in smuggling:

A Cutter supposed to belong to Wm. Dowsett at Paglesham which carries 10 men.

A Cutter supposed to belong to Wiseman of Paglesham which carries 6 men.

A Huffler supposed to belong to the said Dowsett, West Country built, carrying 8 or 9 men.

A smaller boat supposed to belong to Emberson of Paglesham carrying 4 or 5 men.

Another cutter supposed to belong to Adam King, built at Folkestone, carrying 6 or 7 men.

One Cutter supposed to belong to Wm Wright of Burnham called *Sprightly* built in France, Number of hands not known.

That same Maldon Collector also indicted as smugglers 'one or two of the fishing-boats at Burnham which carry oysters to Dunkirk ... [they] frequently run goods in and about Paglesham, Burnham and the creeks adjacent'. Some of these smugglers were sailing their heavily-loaded boats right up the Crouch, even as far as Fambridge Ferry. The newspaper reported in November 1783 that 'a large smuggling vessel mounting several swivels' which was being followed by the Revenue cutter, hit a sandbank below the ferry. The smugglers threw all the contraband overboard and took to their small boat, leaving two men to keep possession of the vessel until it floated off with the tide. From the description it does sound suspiciously like Dowsett's *Big Jane*.

A more violent incident occurred in 1779 when the Revenue cutter *Eagle* challenged a boat trying to smuggle a huge quantity of gin from the port of Flushing, where boats were actually built for this purpose. The smuggler carried 40 men and was armed with 16 carriage guns; it put up a three-hour fight as it retreated through the channels across the sand-banked shallows. One man on the *Eagle* was shot dead, and when the smuggler finally made it to Flushing it was reported that two of its crew had been killed and three injured.

Such incidents did not deter the smugglers, for the large profits to be made were worth the risk of an occasional skirmish. Many of the men had, after all, been brought up on the beach as fishermen's sons and had learned to accept the far greater risks of storms at sea with a stoic indifference. The newspaper reports of clashes and seizures continued, serving to point up the vast amount of goods which were successfully smuggled in. One gang had a system of getting gin ashore and hiding it on Old Hall Marsh at Tollesbury, but they had a setback in 1779 when someone informed on them; the Revenue men from Colchester needed two big wagons to pick up the 210 tubs of gin they found there.

In February 1784 *The Chelmsford Chronicle* reported two

more incidents: 'The revenue officers of Burnham, lately returning with some seized goods, were assaulted by the crews of five free-trading cutters that lay in the river and one of them was dangerously wounded. A few nights before Mr. Francis, an active custom-house officer, master of the "Bull" at Hockley, was attacked and nearly murdered in his own house by a gang of seven daring ruffians, the ringleaders of which declared, they came on purpose to destroy him, but after breaking two of his ribs and giving him several violent contusions on the head, they were prevented from accomplishing their bloody design by the providential arrival of some neighbours, when the villains made their escape hastily; but as they are all known, it is hoped they will soon be apprehended and brought to justice.'

A notice in the *Essex Herald* of 9 February 1808 showed the following in the form of an advertisement: an encounter between smugglers and Revenue men; a successful seizure; and the loss to the smugglers of their means of livelihood, namely their boats. One of them was deliberately sawn in pieces by the Customs officials so that it could not be used again for such nefarious purposes. The advertisement ran:

TO BE SOLD BY AUCTION
By Order of the Honourable the Commissioners of his Majesty's Customs, at the Custom-House at Leigh THE FOLLOWING GOODS:- viz.
  2 Open Boats and Materials
  1 Ditto, Sawn
  2 Warps
  2 Anchors
  1 Cask, quantity two Gallons, Geneva
  19 Yards of Muslin
  29 Yards of Calico
  8 Packages, containing 600lbs. Chinese Vermillion
  30 Gallons Red Port Wine
  38 Bottles ditto
  16 Gallons Rum
  2 Ditto Brandy

1 Mahogany Case, containing six Bottles of Foreign Spiritous Cordials.

To be viewed the day preceeding and morning of the sale, in office hours.

The illicit trade continued, even though an edict was issued in 1785 announcing that any boats which could be classified as 'Cutters, Luggers, Shallops or Wherries' would be confiscated if it could be proved that they had been used for smuggling. The war with France caused some diminution of a trade which had by then become doubly dangerous, but there were still plenty of men who were prepared to take the risks in the hope of making a fortune. The continuing volume of activity can be judged from the fact that James Baxter, Customs officer at Leigh in 1802, noted in his diary that he had made a seizure, large or small, of one kind or another, on each day of the month of July.

A modern writer, James Wentworth Day, describes Leigh, Benfleet and Southend as 'a nest of smugglers, who used church and castle towers as look-out points from which to

Southend in 1898. These locally built vessels are of the same type of which made runs across the channel for supplies of illicit goods.

shine their signals and keep a watch for revenue men'. Leigh's reputation as a haunt of smugglers was supported when the 'Peter Boat' inn was burnt down in 1892. In the ruins was discovered a secret underground room with direct access to the waterfront, and there was some evidence that contraband goods had been stored there.

As soon as the war with France was over the incidence of smuggling increased dramatically, so that in 1816 the government was forced to introduce further 'Laws for the Prevention of Smuggling'. All seamen, guilty or innocent of smuggling, learned that any boat found to be supplied with more than four oars would be confiscated. Other stringent regulations reduced the sail area, speed and size of *any* vessels which could be used for running contraband. Luggers of over 50 tons were totally outlawed. Even signalling from the land to a boat at sea could bring suspicion, arrest and prosecution. A stricter watch was kept along the coast, using several of the war-time Martello towers as observation and rallying points. Men were also quartered in the dismasted hulks of old ships of the line, renamed 'Watch Vessels', so that they could lower boats and row regular patrols of the coastline.

Yet the trade continued. Rowing or pulling boats were secretly made and used. With their shallow draught and their guaranteed power from committed oarsmen they could elude the Revenue cutters time and again. The Revenue cutter *Eagle* was successful in 1818 when it managed to stop a boat pulled by 11 men which was carrying no less than 76 tubs of brandy. Smaller boats were also involved; in the following year the *Eagle* caught one making for the coast with just eight tubs of brandy. The variety of contraband run in this manner is illustrated by the capture of a boat creeping in off Foulness by the *Eagle* and the *Scout* in 1825; on examination the boat proved to be loaded with a cargo of silk.

One of the most resounding successes of the Revenue cutters occurred in December 1849, when the sailing barge *Charlotte*, out of Maldon, was tracked to Gravesend and boarded by a party from the *Vigilant*. It did not need much of a search to discover that the barge was packed with tobacco – nearly six and a half tons of it. It seems likely that the *Vigilant* acted on a tip-off. The Revenue men denied this, but it is 59

The Revenue Cutter *Vigilant* towing a barge seized for carrying contraband tobacco at Greenwich in 1749. (Reproduced by kind permission of Alan Hay)

rather strange that the barge's cabin boy had exactly the same forename and surname as a member of the crew of the *Vigilant*. Each member of that crew stood to gain a proportion of the value of the captured cargo, and the men received £36 each at the final reckoning, while the captain was awarded £540. In today's money that would equal at least £1,000 and £16,000 respectively.

While on station in the Thames in 1871 that same *Vigilant* stopped its namesake, a merchantman out of Rotterdam, but the search produced a mere 119 pounds of tobacco. A great deal of small-scale smuggling was attempted on the side while carrying lawful cargoes, and by this time tobacco was a favourite item in the smuggler's order book. A London tobacco broker declared before the Select Committee on the Tobacco Trade in 1844 that he had heard several reports of wholesale smuggling of tobacco into Essex up the creeks and rivers. As far back as 1833 Essex men had denied such involvement, holding that the notorious Kent and Sussex smugglers had moved in on the Essex coast after being driven from their own areas by the increased vigilance of the local Revenue officers.

But it was a Wivenhoe man, R. Dodds, who in 1833 tried to work the Newcastle-registered brig *Mary* up the Crouch to Battlesbridge with £3,000 worth of tobacco and brandy hidden under a cargo of coal. The chief boatman of the Revenue cutter *Whitworth* was made suspicious by the behaviour of the brig's crew, so it was hailed, halted, boarded and searched. The contraband was found, the crew arrested and the boat seized. The run had been highly organised, for there were horses and carts standing by at Battlesbridge wharf ready to hurry the goods inland. The smugglers were frustrated, but the Revenue men did very nicely out of the value of the boat, its lawful cargo and the contraband. Dodds was found guilty of smuggling, and impressed into the Navy for five years.

The importance of the Blackwater estuary in the story of smuggling is reinforced by the one-time rector of East Mersea, the Rev. Sabine Baring-Gould (1834–1924). He heard all the stories from the old men of the village up to his departure in 1881 and summed them up thus:

'Between Mersea and the Blackwater were several flat

holms or islands, some under water at high tides, others just standing above it, and between these, winding waterways formed a labyrinth which made pursuit difficult. The traffic was carried on with an audacity and openness unparalleled elsewhere. Although there was a coastguard station at the mouth of the estuary on Mersea Hard, yet goods were run even in open day, under the very eyes of the revenue men. Each public house on the island, and on the mainland near a creek, obtained its entire supply of wine and spirits from contraband vessels. Whether the coastguards were bought to shut their eyes or were baffled by the adroitness of the smugglers, cannot be said, but the taverns found no difficulty in obtaining their supplies as often and as abundantly as they desired.

'The villages of Virley and Salcott were the chief landing places and there horses and donkeys were kept in large numbers for the conveyance of the spirits, wine, tobacco and silk to Tiptree Heath, the scene of Boadicea's great battle with the legions of Suetonius, which was the emporium of the trade. There a constant fair or auction of contraband articles went on, and thence they were distributed to Maldon, Colchester, Chelmsford, and even London. Tiptree Heath was a permanent camping ground of gipsies, and there squatters ran up rude hovels; these were all engaged in the distribution of goods brought from the sea.'

As closer watch was kept by the Revenue the smugglers devised more devious ways of getting contraband ashore. A favourite ruse was to sink the goods in well-waterproofed wrappings or containers. The smugglers could mark the spot, but suspicious Revenue men could only cast round the area with grappling irons – an almost hopeless task. Hervey Benham, in his *Once Upon a Tide*, quotes the case of the 16 bales of tobacco, each weighing 40 pounds, found by an Excise officer on a cart standing outside 'The Three Cups' in Springfield (now Chelmsford) in February 1831. On inspection he found they had all been specially wrapped and treated to make them waterproof.

Even later than this we can read of a man who was, by his own admission, a fisherman and a smuggler. William Charles Bradley, born in 1850 at Southend-on-Sea, became an Alder-

63

man on the Borough Council. Secure in that later life of civic dignity he told the story of the day when he sailed as crew for his father on his boat *Quicksilver* in the 1860s. They had been across to Calais, and had picked up quite a cargo of spirits in halfgallon stone bottles. They were optimistically heading for Dover when the Revenue cutter came bearing down upon them. The *Quicksilver* was a fast boat under a big spread of sail. It could have drawn away, but the wind failed them; the Revenue cutter came up, fired a warning shot and lowered a boat with a boarding party. As the oarsmen were pulling across Bill Bradley's father had all the jars brought up on deck as fast as the six crew could carry them, and smashed them all over the side. Everybody had a good swig from the last one before it went overboard. As the Revenue men came aboard they were greeted by the smell of spirits, but nothing could be discovered, though they ripped up floorboards in their frustration. On this occasion the smugglers could notch up a victory over the Customs men, but Bradley's father lost all the money he had invested in that particular cargo.

It seems that by this time, after the reduction of the duty to be paid on so many imports, the trade of smuggling along the coast between the Thames and the Blackwater had been reduced to a kind of adventurous gamble on a cross-Channel sail – the little gamble that is still taken by thousands of travellers returning by flight or ferry with just a little more than their duty-free allowance of alcohol or tobacco.

4

From the Colne to the Stour

A very frustrated Collector of Customs, in charge of the Harwich area in 1777, reported to the Board of Commissioners that he 'had been informed that there are upwards of 30 sail of small cutters constantly employed in smuggling between the Naze point and the mouth of the Thames, which vessels easily elude the pursuit of the "Argus" and the "Bee" cutters stationed at this port by running over the sands where on account of their great draft of water those cutters dare not follow, by which means they escape and carry on with impunity a great trade in the rivers and creeks which abound in these parts'.

This passage sums up the lie of the land between the Colne and the Stour. The river Colne winds south-east to the sea from Colchester, capital of The Ancient Britons. On its way it receives tribute from the Roman River, Alresford Creek, Geedon Creek, Pyefleet Channel, Flag Creek, Brightlingsea Creek and St Osyth Creek, before joining the estuary of the Blackwater between Mersea Flats and Colne Point.

The Custom House on Colchester Quay was the home base of the local Customs cutter, and though not all the records they kept have survived one can still read the letters sent to the Collector at Colchester from the Board of Commissioners for Customs in London. The Collector was responsible for organising regular patrols of a long stretch of coast to intercept smugglers before they could make a landing. That we have even these records is entirely due to the enthusiasm of a former librarian and archivist of H.M. Customs and Excise. Back in 1923 he carefully copied the surviving records and made a typed transcript. In the Second World War the original

Places associated with smuggling in North Essex.

documents were totally destroyed, but copies of the typed transcript survived.

Mersea was cut off from the mainland by the Mersea Fleet, the Strood Channel and the Byfleet Channel, but connected at low tide by the Strood, a causeway built by the Romans. On the seaward side of the island the mudflats running round from West to East Mersea gave smugglers every opportunity to run their boats up the gently-sloping beach. Across the Colne estuary the St Osyth marshes ran on east in watery remoteness. Lee Wick, Wigboro Wick, Seawick, Cockett Wick and Jaywick were a string of outlying farms with their own secret paths through the marshes to the beach. The seamarks here were the tower and the spire of St Osyth and Clacton churches and, later, the Martello towers built right on the

66

The sands and low cliffs of North Essex. Small smuggling boats could reach the safety of the secluded creeks because the large Custom and Excise Cutters were unable to pursue them inshore.

coast between the two villages to deter any projected French invasion at the end of the 18th century.

From Clacton through Frinton to Walton with its Naze, the low cliffs faced the eroding fury of the winter-rough North Sea. Even here, though, there were gaps where the marshes drained to the sea, which provided useful access inland for goods landed on the beach. Holland Haven where the Holland Brook falls into the North Sea is a good example. Beyond it, and beyond the cliffs of Frinton and Walton, is the headland of the Naze. On this eminence, in 1720, Trinity House had a tower built specially to serve as a seamark for shipping – very helpful to a smuggler creeping in.

North of the Naze, Hamford Water runs inland from Penny-   67 hole Bay, almost isolating the Naze and forming Peewit, Skipper, Horsey and Hedge-End islands. On a dark night the shallow creeks provided countless opportunities to run a boat up Kirby Creek and the Wade to Marsh House and Birch Hall. To the west Beaumont Quay did genuine trade during the day and contraband by night, with easy access to the high road, now the A136, which led to Harwich in one direction and Colchester in the other.

Little Oakley lies inland, just beyond the marshes which eventually give way to the buildings of modern Dovercourt and old Harwich. From Harwich the packet-boats which carried the mail provided a regular link with the Low Countries and the German states, and there were plenty of examples of smuggling by crews and passengers.

The relatively good lines of communication based on old Roman roads allowed swift passage south-west to London. The building of the railway along a similar line after 1840 made the transport of considerable loads of contraband even simpler, although it also gave the opportunity for closer control over its movements. The big railway ferry terminus was developed at Parkeston Quay west of Harwich on the estuary of the Stour which until that time was a lonely, marshy spot very suitable for the landing of the odd parcel of silk or lace and a cask or two of spirits.

The Stour is a Suffolk river, rising over to the west near Newmarket, but it runs on to form the boundary with Essex all the way to its broad estuary, forming the delightful scenery forever to be remembered as 'Constable Country'. In 1706 the Stour was developed as a waterway for transport and could be used from the port of Manningtree, where the river is a mile across, right up to Sudbury.

All this area of coast and estuaries and offshore shallows was watched over by the Riding Officers, Revenue sloops, Tide Surveyors, Searchers, Boatmen and others under the supervision of the Collectors at Colchester and at Harwich. Some of the problems of enforcing the payment of duty are indicated in the stream of directives which flowed from the Board of Commissioners in London to its hard-pressed Collector at Colchester from 1729 to the end of the century. The

68

Collector's replies and reports have, unfortunately, been lost through enemy action and the passage of time, but the correspondence he received has been preserved.

The escalation of the war between smugglers and Revenue men is apparent from the very first item of business recorded, in which the Collector is asking for the repayment of £5.3s.0d. which he had paid out for medical attention to three men for the injuries they had received at the hands of the smugglers. Reading between the lines, this entry connects with the conviction at Chelmsford Assizes in January 1730 of James Barr, John Gooding and James Bentley on a charge of 'obstructing Thomas Nichols and Edward Moseley, Riding Officers and their assistant in the execution of their duty on 15th December, 1727'.

The Revenue men could give as good as they got. John Aldis, a smuggler, had his leg broken in a clash, was captured, sentenced and confined in Chelmsford Gaol. Injured and penniless, he turned evidence for the Crown and received an allowance of three shillings and sixpence a week from the Board of Customs as an informer. But he had already incurred a debt of some six pounds for medical attention. He made a pathetic appeal to the Board and they doubled his weekly allowance, on the condition that he paid off the debt in regular instalments.

Smuggler John Sampson did not get off so well. He was not injured when captured but caught a fever soon after and had to be looked after locally until he was well enough to be taken to prison. The Board was concerned as to how it could get Sampson to repay the ten pounds it cost them to keep him whilst in their custody.

Some encouragement to face and capture smugglers was given by the offer in 1720 of rewards for the arrest of smugglers who were subsequently convicted. On 25 June 1734, Isaac Decker, 'on board the sloop in the service at your Port', asked for a reward under the Act (6 George I) for arresting Emanuel Grootham, 'one of the smugglers concerned in assaulting Captain Martin in May 1729'. The Board had to point out that, according to the Act, the £40 reward was not to be paid out unless at least two offenders from any particular gang were

69

Hythe Quay, Colchester in 1900. In the heyday of smuggling vast numbers of barges and boats used the wharves here.

convicted. But they nevertheless so appreciated Decker's efforts on this occasion that they told the Collector at Colchester to pay him £20.

The apprehension of smugglers became quite a profitable business for Mr William Lisle, Supervisor of the Riding Officers based on Colchester. On 7 August 1734 he wrote to the Board in London, via the Colchester Collector, asking for a reward for the capture of five smugglers – John Ames, Edward Spells, John Thurgood, William Mayes and Philip Farrington. This request was probably a result of an announcement by the Board in 1728 that it would give a reward for information leading to the arrest of a gang of some 40 smugglers who, caught red-handed in making a landing off Clacton, beat off and badly injured the Riding Officers there. Lisle suggested to the Board that he be given £12 for each man captured and that future arrests be rewarded at the same rate. He told the Board that he in return would personally pay his informers and also the costs of the Dragoons he might need to escort the smugglers to gaol. The Board, rather unusually, agreed to this arrangement, but insisted that he render an account of his expenses to the Collector.

That Collector certainly had a multitude of duties to perform. First and foremost he had to arrange for all the dues to be collected from law-abiding merchants and contractors all around his stretch of the coast. The prevention of smuggling and the seizure of contraband was an unenviable extra task which created its own pile of paperwork. Take the case of Thomas Streaton who was appointed as a Riding Officer at Colchester in 1735. He asked for an annual allowance of £10 to keep his horse. It parallels the car allowance claimed by many an executive today. The Collector agreed, but had to write to the Board for authority. The Board made it more complicated for him. 'You are to see that the said Streaton rides the coast and does the duty for which the said allowance was made and at the end of twelve months report what services he has performed. You are also, in conjunction with the Supervisor of the Riding Officers, to prepare proper instructions for the said Streaton so far as relates to his duty of riding the coast and transmit the same for our approbation.'

All this paperwork was necessary to the proper administration of a nationally organised department of the Government. When Lambe Wigmore, employed in the service as a boatman at Brightlingsea, had been put on the *Friendly Love*, loaded with timber from Norway, to make sure there was no clandestine unloading of any dutiable goods, he deserted his post under cover of darkness and went ashore to more comfortable lodgings. His absence was discovered when Mr Todd the Surveyor paid the ship a surprise visit. Wigmore was docked a fortnight's wages to teach him a lesson and Mr Leach, Paymaster of the Superannuation Fund, was to be informed.

This humble example demonstrates the difficulties and the determination of the Colchester Collector to run his region effectively. He was himself rapped over the knuckles when he allowed Edward Moseley, one of the Clacton Riding Officers, to have six days' special leave without attempting to cover for his absence. The Board was severe: 'You are to give orders to the neighbouring officers that they extend and alter their rides so that the District of the said Moseley may be guarded and that the Service may not suffer.'

While the Riding Officers, if they were diligent, had a difficult job patrolling their area in good weather and bad, and

mostly at night, the Revenue boats had an even more dis-
agreeable time of it. With wind and oar as the only means of
propulsion and manoeuvre, and with the ever-changing mood
of the sea to contend with, an encounter with armed smugglers
could be nightmarish. In 1738 Captain Robert Martin was
contracting one of his several boats, the *Princess Mary*, with its
crew, to the Service at an agreed rate quarterly of thirty
shillings per ton of a sloop which was 67 tons burthen. It had
to be armed owing to the fact that the smugglers' craft were
specially built for their purpose and were themselves heavily
armed. In 1740 six guns on carriages were mounted in the
Princess Mary, and in June of the following year Martin took on
eight more crew, 'in order the better to enable him to attack
the outlaws and other notorious smugglers'. The record shows
that their pay, at £18 a year, far exceeded that of a farm
worker or servant. What is more, the seamen stood to benefit
from any seizures the sloop might make. But there was always
the risk of death to consider. In January 1743 the Collector
had to report the death of John Miles in a rowing boat, 'shot
by smugglers while endeavouring to seize their goods'.

Renewed hostilities with France and Spain in 1745 brought
further problems, not just for the Colchester Collector but for
the whole service. All the Custom House sloops were immediately put under the direction of the Lords of the Admiralty
and 'the Commanders of Customs Vessels stationed on the
Coast of Norfolk, Suffolk and Essex and in the River of
Thames' were ordered 'to repair to the Nore and follow such
order as they shall receive from Commodore Smith or Capt.
Boscawen ... The Commissioners direct you immediately to
acquaint Captain Martin, Commander of the Custom House
Sloop at your Port therewith ... and he is to give an account of
all his proceedings whilst he is on this service'.

Within eleven days, on 17 December 1745, the Customs
officers had another huge task laid upon them. They had to
prevent from leaving port all ships laden with 'black cattle and
hogs, beef, pork, butter and cheese'. This was because, at this
time of crisis, several ships of the Royal Navy were unable to
sail to their action stations because they did not have enough
supplies, either on board or at the victualling yards, to feed
their crews.

Wivenhoe, where many of the Revenue Cutters were based, this being the furthest they could proceed up the river Colne.

Time, as usual, took care of the crisis and after three years almost to the day the Commissioners, ever with an eye to economy, were able to issue the edict that 'Having taken into consideration the great charge the Crown has been put to by the number of additional mariners employed on board the several sloops in the service of the Customs in order to defend them as well against small privateers as the large arm'd smuglers, and being of opinion as the War is over that they are become unnecessary, we have therefore thought fit to direct that the eight additional mariners allowed the Commander of the sloop at your Port from 9th June 1741 be discharged at Christmas next.'

Royal Naval ships had increased in number during the war, and on their travels they had collected 'great quantities of goods as well Customable as prohibited and run them on the Coasts . . . of this Kingdom'. This was yet another problem for the Collectors, who were ordered to inform the commanders of all boats in their ports, large or small, which were employed in

73

any way by the Royal Navy that this did not 'exempt their being rummaged by the officers of His Majesty's Customs'. By 1751 the incidence of smuggling was so widespread that the Board of Commissioners wrote to their Colchester Collector, telling him to alert and invigorate his officers and men to greater effort because 'great quantities of goods are almost daily run on your coast, particularly tobacco stalks'. Their concern was timely, for in the following year there is a record of a seizure of a hundredweight of cut tobacco stalks, 1023 lbs of roll tobacco and 22,782 lbs of damaged tobacco stalks. All were burnt, and Captain Martin and his crew shared a reward of £103.18s.4d. which was computed on the basis of the value of the goods seized.

In January 1754 one of the Colchester sloops made another big seizure: over 14 tons of stalk and rolled tobacco given up without a fight. The profit to the smuggler on any one run was sufficient to allow him to shrug off even such a loss as this, on occasion. The intrepid Captain Martin, meanwhile, had moved on from merely commanding a Revenue sloop to appointment, in about 1740, as Surveyor of Sloops for the East Coast. There was only one other such appointment in the whole country. He had grown in status and wealth, contracting to supply five ships, with crews, for the Colchester area and a couple at Harwich. The *Princess Mary* which he started with in 1729 was rebuilt in 1747, and the record of seizures shows how it carried on the good work.

Kenneth Walker, writing the History of Clacton in 1966, made a good point when he came to the period in which smuggling was at its height: 'Great Clacton became a centre of smuggling, many a load of contraband being landed on its desolate beach. Farm workers, and indeed most of its inhabitants, were probably involved in this illicit trafficking. Taking their horses, or those of their employers (who were suitably rewarded), they stole by night down to the shore where they unloaded the spirits, silks, tobacco and other goods, and conveyed them to their cottages.' Apparently they were given instructions to rendezvous a night or two later when the smugglers collected the contraband and arranged for its onward transmission to Colchester and other centres of shops and markets right down to London.

That the Riding Officers and the seaborne patrols were not equal to the occasion in the first quarter of the 18th century is evident from the reward offered in a newspaper in 1728 for 'the apprehension of a gang of 30 to 40 smugglers, who had violently beaten and wounded a Riding Officer and Constable at the Port of London when discharging their duty on the coast of Clackton'.

In another incident a gang of smugglers overwhelmed a posse of Customs officers and held them prisoner while they made a big landing of tea, then released them in a gesture of contemptuous magnanimity. And it was not long after these reverses that a Revenue cutter trying to prevent a smuggling lugger from approaching the shore to make a landing was met with such a fusillade that it had to break off and stand out to sea.

The Revenue men suffered a more domestic defeat at the hands of old Dawson and his wife who lived in a cottage in Old Road. As late in the history of smuggling as 1832 Dawson had got himself involved in a landing, and had his share safely stored at home. But somebody had split on this particular operation and the Revenue men were on their way to round up the smugglers. Dawson had just enough time to hide his haul under the bed in which his wife was about to go to sleep. He whispered her a few urgent words – and when the officers of the Revenue banged hard upon the door he welcomed them to search the house, but begged them to be as quiet as possible because his wife was very ill indeed in the room above. When one of them put his foot on the ladder which stood for a staircase Mrs Dawson cried out as if in her last extremities. Dawson darted forward, declared his wife was dying and he must go up to her at once. The Revenue men, nonplussed, made a discreet departure.

Smugglers were not a race apart; they and their customers ranged through every rank of society. It was normally only the desperation of imminent capture which led to impulsive violence. Life was so hard, so basic in those unlettered days that no comparison can be made with the desperadoes of our day. Smugglers were the Robin Hoods of the 18th century; they brought goods into the country at a reasonable price which the less well-off could afford. The illiterate people who helped

75

them knew nothing of the costs of wars, the expense of government. They did know they were paid handsomely for their assistance. Over a glass or two of their illicit liquor smugglers would be as cheerful and friendly as the stagecoach driver or the postboy.

Some of them must have had a certain sense of humour when, in 1744, they carried off William Lisle, Supervisor of Riding Officers at Colchester Custom House and, as we have seen, an energetic arrester of smugglers. They kidnapped him, but did him no harm, releasing him on extracting his promise that he would not reveal their identities. They were daring too, for when some seven tons of tea had been seized from a boat in 1748 a gang of about 30 smugglers broke into the Colchester Custom House store, threatened the officers and retrieved their cargo almost as soon as it had been unloaded there.

Some people, including the Harwich Collector, strongly suspected that William Lisle had something to do with the smugglers' success in this episode. The Collector had been at loggerheads with Lisle for years over the latter's methods of capturing individual smugglers for personal gain and getting them 'turned round' and paid as informers. Captain Martin, Controller of the Revenue cutters at Colchester and at Harwich, was said to back the Harwich Collector, and since the possibility of collusion in the service was like the rotten apple in the barrel, Lisle was suspended in 1750 and asked to return his commission.

The extent of the smugglers' success can be judged by the amounts of contraband seized, for they formed a very small proportion of the total amount of goods run on to the east coast. That is why the smugglers were encouraged to continue their trade. The newspapers of the time report sales like that at Wivenhoe in 1743 when the auction of seized contraband included 'neat old Bordeaux and Nantes brandies', totalling an amazing 5,900 gallons. The *Chelmsford Chronicle* of 16 August 1776 carried the advertisement:

'To be SOLD to the BEST BIDDER (By INCH of CANDLE) on Tuesday the 20th August, 1776, at the CUS-TOM HOUSE in COLCHESTER, upwards of Two Thousand Gallons foreign Brandy, One Thousand Two Hundred and Twenty-two Pounds Black Tea, and Two Hundred and Two Pounds Green Tea; also a quantity of strong spirits.'

In 1787 other seizures put on sale included over 1500 gallons of Geneva, Rum and Brandy as well as wine, tea – even soap and starch. The duty on soap had been introduced in 1712 and continued until 1835.

That the variety of items on which duty was charged was extremely wide is illustrated by the unusual request made by the Collector in November 1770 that he be allowed to buy a small, old boat which could be loaded with fifty bundles of hemp, then ballasted and sunk in deep water. The hemp had been discovered floating in the Wallet – a channel off the Blackwater estuary – by William Cole, master of a fishing vessel out of Wivenhoe. It was just the kind of contraband which could be sunk with weights in shallow water and 'crept' for later with a grapnel. This was a system which in later, less violent days of smuggling was particularly appropriate to the sandy shallows around the Essex coast. The Board helped their hard-pressed Collector by enquiring round and finding that Captain Harvey, Commander of the Revenue cutter *Earl of Rochford* based in the Collector's own port, knew of an old, condemned boat which could be made ready for such use at a cost of just forty shillings.

Contraband which reached dry land and the high road could still be apprehended. In January 1772 the Excise officer at Brentwood got wind of a smugglers' convoy heading for London through Billericay, and called on the army for assistance. So it was that, with a recruiting sergeant and three of his recruits of the 24th Regiment of Foot, the Excise man sallied forth, rather unwisely, to confront a vastly superior number of armed smugglers escorting 20 horses loaded with contraband. The *Ipswich Journal* takes up the story: 'The supervisor presented a pistol at one of the smugglers who in a sneering manner had him put it up . . . the smugglers . . . went through Brentwood in triumph about two, and were seen to go through Ilford about four. One of the smugglers received a violent cut with a sword on the side of his head which almost took off his cheek.' The sergeant probably did that – in return he was wounded in six places: 'The supervisor is dangerously wounded and his recovery is doubtful and one of the recruits is likely to lose his arm.'

The Excise officers must have been tipped off to search the Ipswich-bound coach at Colchester for, as reported by the

Walton on the Naze in 1895. The same kind of boats used in the smuggling trade are still in use today, now in the tourist trade.

local paper in February 1777 they found 'a box of cambrick, containing 112 pieces and sundry bags of fine teas packed up in boxes and hampers; the quantity of tea was upwards of 3 cwt'. The report added 'They are directed to persons of quality', which puts the whole business almost on a footing with the mail-order business of today.

It was not surprising that the number of Revenue cutters based on Colchester was increased. One name famous among them was *Repulse* which was used down the years for six craft in succession: from that built in 1774, crewed by 11 men and a boy, to the sixth in the line which carried a crew of 37 and was still sailing in 1821.

The Colchester cutters were based at Wivenhoe, this being the furthest they could proceed up the Colne. This port bred two cutter captains of particularly rugged character.

From as early as 1698 there was a boat known and hated by frustrated smugglers as the 'Wivenhoe Smack', and its name was used for the boat commissioned in 1731, supplied on a contract basis by Robert Martin who also acted as its captain.

He had started with the 67-ton *Essex* and the 73-ton *Princess Mary*, both stationed at Wivenhoe under the Colchester Collector from 1729 to 1741. From time to time they were seconded to other stations.

The house where he lived at this time is still standing on the quay at Rowhedge on the other bank of the Colne, for it has been identified as 3, High Street, on the corner of Darkhouse Lane. At the peak of his career in the service Martin was contracting eight ships to patrol from Colchester, Harwich and the Medway. He took personal command of the *Princess Mary* from 1740 and had her rebuilt and increased in size in 1747. By the following year he was prosperous enough to buy the Manor of Great Holland, near Clacton. He died in 1764, but not before he saw his daughter married to John Kirby, the Colchester Collector.

He was succeeded by Daniel Harvey, who had been Captain of the *Princess Mary* from 1760. He was a man cast in Martin's mould and soon made his mark with that line of *Repulse* Revenue cutters, personally commanding the first four. The fourth was probably the biggest of all the Revenue cutters built in the 18th century, carrying a crew of 50 men plus the inevitable cabin boy. Harvey took out a licence to use the *Repulse* in his own time, and at his own expense, as a privateer – and had some strange adventures. The sixth and last *Repulse*, which carried a crew of 37 and was much smaller, carried on the record of service down to 1813, when it was moved to Grimsby.

As Graham Smith says in his *King's Cutters* 'many of the developments in small vessel and yacht design can be traced to the Revenue cutters of the late eighteenth and early nineteenth century'. They had their successes, as proved by paragraphs in the papers such as that in the *Essex Chronicle* of 12 October 1764: 'Harwich ... Monday. The Custom-house smack, Captain Dagnett, took a smuggling cutter with brandy and geneva on-board, and brought her into our harbour. The *Hector* cutter has likewise taken a smuggling cutter, and carried her into Brightlinsea.'

They had their reverses of fortune as well. It appears that late in 1777 James Woodward, master of the *Swift* cutter, and his crew had caught a smuggling cutter at sea. They had

The tower on the Naze, erected as a landmark for shipping.

stopped it, discovered its cargo of contraband tea and had officially 'seized' it when the smugglers, chief of whom were John Ward, Isaac Johnson, Sapperton Sallowes, William Watson, Samuel Fryer and Thomas Buck, turned the tables on them, overpowered the crew, whom they outnumbered, and regained possession of their cutter and their tea. They also took Woodward and four of his crew hostage. The record does not tell us just how they were set on shore again.

This was a humiliation for the service and it seems that the Commissioners suspected some laxity in the outports. On 15 August 1780 they thundered: 'The Board having given the greatest encouragement to the several Waterguard officers of this Revenue by furnishing them with cruisers built upon the very best construction and in many instances also by increasing the tonnage and number of men whereby the Revenue has been put to a very considerable expense and having nevertheless strong reason to believe that the standing orders of this Board for the diligent and effectual exertion of such cruisers have not been duly obey'd we think it necessary to remind and enjoin you to pay a strict attention thereto.'

The smugglers appeared to have had the whip hand, landing most of their goods at will. Within 18 months the Board was further castigating its officers: 'The enormous increase in smuggling, the outrages with which it is carried on, the mischief it occasions to the country, the discouragement it creates to all fair traders and the prodigious loss the revenue sustains by it call upon us to repeat and enforce the means which appear to us likely if duly executed to give a check to this national evil. Diligent and vigorous exertions by the Cruising Vessels employed in the service of the Customs certainly might very much lessen it and therefore we cannot but reflect with much dissatisfaction on the want of success which has attended our endeavours to render the Waterguard in general much more efficacious than it has hitherto proved, a Defect which we believe could not have happened if the instructions and orders given by this Board had been duly observed.'

The Board's bark was worse than its bite. In just three months Mr Munday, Surveyor to the Board, was reporting great satisfaction with every aspect of the management of the

An early Victorian sketch of the Suffolk coast in smuggling times.

Port of Colchester, and those Customs officers still had something to contend with. On the one hand distilleries had been
set up at Schiedam especially to supply the British smugglers
with gin. By 1779 they could produce four million gallons a
year. English entrepreneurs, settled along the coast from
France to Holland, arranged for its reception at ports like
Flushing and its collection by the smuggling concerns. The
smugglers' ships then fanned out across the Channel heading
for their local areas, where they could run their cargoes on the
beach or make rendezvous with local boats prepared to make
individual runs. On the other hand special smuggling craft
were being built on those same foreign shores to outwit the
government regulations on size and sail power, and these craft
were well able to beat the Revenue cutters for speed.

The idea of using multi-oared rowing boats to bring contraband across from the Continent, especially on the shorter
Channel trips, was early taken up. Such boats did not have to
wait for the wind and they showed a very low profile to the
look-out on the Revenue cutter or on the headland. They
could also very easily be run through the shallows and straight
up the beach. Customs officers, however, were not slow to
appreciate and act upon this situation. They got the Govern-

Harwich from the sea in 1830.

ment to ban from the south-east coast any boat equipped to be propelled by more than four oars. In 1779 this ban was extended to East Anglia in respect of boats with more than six oars, but from 1818 the Essex Revenue men could confiscate any boat they found with more than four oars. The length of such boats had also been restricted to 14 feet. By 1826, after much flouting of the regulations, it was laid down that all owners had to obtain a licence for their boats, and that open boats of this nature were not allowed to cross the Channel. Many more regulations were promulgated at this time concerning craft of all kinds, in further efforts to reduce smuggling. The fact that they were integrated and reinforced in 1841 shows that smuggling continued to be a problem for the Treasury and a headache for the Colchester Collector.

Life for the smuggler was made more uninviting when, by a law introduced in 1833, a term of imprisonment could include hard labour. In 1831 Thomas Wright, the Essex historian, wrote with pride of the new gaol at Chelmsford where prisoners, including smugglers, were put to work in the treadmill which ground the flour for their bread. One such prisoner was Thomas Bacon. He was stopped in an open boat heading for the Crouch with no less than 150 casks of spirits, and he ended up in that new gaol.

By comparison the crew of the *Rover*, a type of rowing galley, were lucky. Chased by a Coastguard boat, they made it to the shore and unloaded 160 barrels into a ditch, the best hiding-place to hand. Then they scattered inland, and got away. Meanwhile the Coastguards followed their footprints to the ditch, and added their booty to another of those Custom House sales. One held in the same year as this capture, 1832, included no less than 91 lots of all kinds of contraband, showing that the men of the Colchester area were making their mark in the struggle against the 'Free Traders'. By 1840 there had been established a very popular and convenient sale of contraband which took place annually just prior to Christmas.

Increasingly the smugglers fell back on the less easily detectable practice of dropping weighted contraband over-board by night in the shallows just offshore, either in 'tubs' for spirits, or in waterproofed wrappings for a remarkable variety of other goods.

5
From the Orwell to the Alde

The lie of the land on the Essex side of the great, wide estuary formed by the junction of the Stour and the Orwell in Harwich Harbour has already been described. It will feature again, because the Harwich cutters and Riding Officers patrolled up and down the coast either side of the port. They might have expected some assistance in their efforts, for on the eastern side of the harbour the long promontory tipped by Landguard Point sticks out into the North Sea, and on its remote and low-lying common lay the great fort which helped secure the safety of the port in time of war.

In fact when it came to action against armed smugglers, the military were not very co-operative. In 1739, when the Harwich Collector wanted help in trying to stop a ship, the *Middleburg Merchant*, from sailing away against an order of restraint with two of his men still on board, the sergeant at the fort was no help at all. He simply said that his superior officer had given orders that the Collector should not be assisted, and that was that. This may have been because of an incident earlier in the year. The Collector, ordered by the Board to draw up a new chart for the harbour, was rowed across the harbour to the fort, complete with his measuring instruments. He asked the Deputy Governor for permission to measure that side of the harbour, taking bearings on the churches in Harwich. The Deputy Governor treated him as no more than a spy come to measure the very fortifications themselves, seized his instruments, bundled him unceremoniously out of the fort and sent a letter of complaint direct to the Treasury. There was obviously no love lost between the Revenue men and the military.

Places associated with smuggling in South Suffolk.

From the harbour there was much coming and going on the Orwell, to and from the Port of Ipswich. The wherries, deep-laden as barges and sailing as slowly, were a vital part of the trade. This was another port through which wool was smuggled out of the country from the earliest times. In 1784 there was sold at a Customs auction at Mistley Thorn 48 bags of raw wool which some hapless speculator had hoped to smuggle abroad for a good profit. Even in the first part of the 19th century crewels, the fine worsted yarn made in Suffolk, and much prized on the Continent, was going down to Harwich for onward carriage as contraband. Meanwhile a much greater volume and variety of imported goods, on which duty should

86

have been paid, found its way up the reaches and the channels of the Orwell to Cliff Quay and the docks at Ipswich.

The establishment of customs duty on imports at Ipswich can be dated back to the 14th century, judging by the architecture of the original Custom House. This was demolished in 1844 but drawings still exist. It was replaced by the Town House, which cost £5,000 in the money of the day, and was designed by J. M. Clarke to accommodate both Customs and Excise departments. The Ipswich Dock Company took it over in 1920 when the Customs office moved to Museum Street.

Further north and east a great parallelogram of land is enclosed between the Orwell the Deben and the sea, where Felixstowe has grown in recent times into a large container-handling port. The Deben meanders down from Woodbridge (which had its own Custom House) with the Fynn feeding it through Martlesham Creek just below the little town. A line drawn due east on the map would pass through Rendlesham Forest above Woodbridge Airfield to meet the sea at Orford, crossing the Butley river to Orford and Orford Ness. There, behind the long, gravelly bank of Orford Beach, the Alde runs parallel with the sea for miles to join with the Ore past Havergate Island and to run on again for some three miles before turning out to the sea at Oxley Marshes and North Weir Point.

This then was the area in which the Harwich Collector had to deploy his pitifully small army to overcome the determined and violent assaults of the smugglers on the Suffolk shore. He had a far more difficult assignment than either of his neighbours at Colchester and Yarmouth, because he had to deal with the packet boats coming into Harwich – the captains and crews of which could be cunning, argumentative and obdurate. Sailing as regularly as wind and weather would allow these ferry boats had constant contact with Continental ports. The sailors were not particularly well paid, and many were tempted to bring in any dutiable items which could be sold for a handsome profit.

As far back as 1714, on 22 July, the Collector had to report to the Board of Commissioners for Customs in London that 'Yesterday Mr Lowndes seized out of the "Dolphin" Pacquet boat about forty five gallons Brandy, Nine gallons spirits, five

87

The second Ipswich Custom House, built in the 1840s following the construction of the new wet dock. (Reproduced by kind permission of The Suffolk Record Office)

small baggs nutt-meggs, a paper parcell cloves, four pieces of lutestring, one peece alamode, three peeces course Dutch whrought mantua silk and one remnant of Dutch printed callicoe; the said silks were found concealed in the side of the forecastle of the vessel, to come at which a plank was taken out.' The wide range of goods on which tax was levied could not be better illustrated. We have it on Graham Smith's authority in *King's Cutters* that this was the earliest example of smuggling by concealment rather than by the usual method then of unloading goods quite openly on the beach.

The packet boats were not above sinking contraband, particularly tubs of spirits, just outside the harbour for collection at some convenient time by a small boat. In 1718 the Collector proposed to the Board that 'a pinnace to be commanded and managed by the Tydesurveyer of this port will be altogether as effectual [as a smack or yacht] to prevent the too common and pernicious practice of the pacquet boats sinking brandy and other prohibited goods without the Harbour on the return from Holland as well as unfair traders from France doing the like'. It does not appear that the threat represented by this pinnace deterred the crew of the packet boat *Dispatch*, for when Customs officer Whitcomb searched it in 1721 he brought to light four gallons of spirits, 15½ yards of Dutch printed calico and eight pounds of pepper. He would have been roundly cursed by the crew.

The passengers on the packet boats were also under suspicion, and on occasion this had curious consequences. In 1752 a Miss de Bardieux, arriving at Harwich from Holland, had some parcels taken off her as containing dutiable goods which she was smuggling in. She wrote to the Customs authority asking for the return of these goods and complaining that she was treated with great indecency by the officers of the Customs. The Harwich Collector, called on to explain, 'found that there were no indecencys acted but by herself for when the tyde-surveyor found she had something concealed in her stays, she took him round the neck and held and kiss'd him a considerable time in the presence of several people. And when Mr. Orlibar & Mr. Pulham went to her to the Publick House and acquainted her they had information that she had some prohibited goods concealed about her, she immediately lifted up her petticoats up to her waist so that her whole behaviour here was very like a common strumpet'.

A record of 20 years later shows that a gentleman tried to bring in two valuable snuffboxes via the packet boat by putting each in a leather bag tied in his manservant's breeches, 'next to his backside'. Apparently this was a method of smuggling so widely used that the Customs officer rumbled it at once. On the sea crossing even King's Messengers were not above using their office to deceive the Customs. One who was stopped at Harwich in 1746 had put fine linen in a parcel sealed and addressed to His Majesty's Secretary. 'After this detection,' said the Collector, 'no-one can wonder how the millinery shops in London came to be filled with prohibited Dresden needlework.' It makes the point nicely that the protection of British trade as well as loss of government revenue could be jeopardised by the huge volume of goods then being smuggled. Leonard Weaver, in *The Harwich Story*

(1975) puts a further point: 'it should be noted that the view of smugglers as being romantic heroes bears little relation to the facts. During the wars with France there were many cases reported from Harwich where smugglers had been caught helping the enemy in return for contraband and money.'

As a packet port Harwich saw a great influx of refugees from the French Revolution, and many were anxious to bring in a few treasured possessions. But the rule was that packet boats must convey nothing but the mails, and passengers with their baggage, and that must exclude anything dutiable. Souvenirs and personal treasures were 'mercilessly seized' – often because the officer seizing them stood to receive half the sale value realised at the next Custom House auction. This arrangement certainly encouraged attention to duty but, as can be imagined, it also brought about a good deal of corruption.

In the town of Harwich itself smugglers were insolently, overtly active. Imagine the scene at ten o'clock on the night of 9 October 1714. Thomas Cribband, Tidesman, and William Whitehead, Boatman, were sent into the town on patrol. In a yard in West Street they found five half-ankers of brandy. There were the two men, all alone out in the dark, wondering what to do about this unwelcome discovery when 'four persons unknown on horse back and one or two on foot, armed with clubbs and other weapons who were to convey the said brandy out of the Towne, assisted by James Mortlock, employed in the lighthouse here, furiously assaulted the officers, beating and wounding them inhumanely and forced out of their possession three of the said casks and rode off with them after which the said Mortlock constrained Wm. Whitehead into a house where the said Mortlock beat him unmercifully that murther was cried out which it is believed the said Mortlock had perpetrated if one Thomas Boucher a taylor had not prevented him by rescuing Whitehead out of his hands. About the beginning of the fray, Jeremy Malden, one of the constables of this corporation was called to use his authority for assisting the officers and to keep the peace, who refused so doing and said he had no warrant but continued present and seemed very well pleased to see the officers barbarously used'. Without the help of the troops in the fort and the constables in the town the

A   B

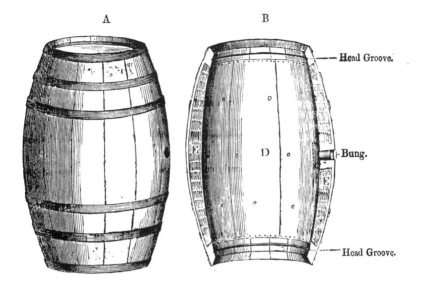

Head Groove.

Bung.

Head Groove.

C

A.—Section of Cask in its original state.

B.—Section of half the Cask cut from head to head.

C.—Section of Cask cut transversely.

D.—The Tin lining.

E.—The space between the Tin lining and the Cask in which the Segars were secreted.

Diagram showing how cigars were hidden in barrels. (Reproduced by kind permission of H.M. Commissioners of Customs and Excise)

91

Harwich Collector was fighting crime with both arms tied behind his back.

Smuggling was so open that Captain Phillips, commanding one of the Revenue vessels, was able to make a seizure of goods landed for later collection simply by following the tracks of a wagon up the shore. The lack of sufficient officers made adequate coverage of the whole coast by land or sea quite impossible and the smugglers took great advantage of that fact. They also had the majority of local people on their side; the upper classes liked the lower prices of untaxed luxury items and the working men welcomed the reward, in money or in kind, which they could earn by giving a little help on a dark night.

By 1716 the Customs service was getting better organised; the Collector at Harwich had defined the problem: that between Harwich and Colchester he had no officers deployed except two Boatmen at Brightlingsea, up the river Colne, and they were of no use at all on the long stretch of coast that came under his jurisdiction. Then he put forward his suggestion that, if two Riding Officers were appointed and stationed at Walton, at a salary of £50 each, they could check the coast in both directions as they would be equidistant from the two ports of Colchester and Harwich, and they could 'correspond with and be assisting Mr. David Rushton, officer at Manytree [Manningtree]'. The Board approved and two men, D'Oyley and Eslyn, were soon appointed.

It was Rushton who, in September 1721, found just one half-anker sized cask of brandy on the beach. Evidence of operations on a much larger scale was found in the same month by Mr D'Oyley, who discovered 19 half-ankers of brandy hidden underground at Frinton by the simple process of falling through the frail covering of the hole. The following December found Captain Phillips at sea using his telescope to keep an eye on some suspicious activity of men in a marsh near Kirby-le-Soken. He waited until they departed, then pulled in to the shore and found 54 half-ankers of brandy hurriedly buried in three different places. Since he and his crew would have a share of the proceeds when the brandy was sold at the next Custom House auction sale, they could look forward to an enriching new year.

In the following year, 1722, it was reported of D'Oyley that he frequently met smugglers 'who ride with goods in great partys, consisting of twenty, thirty and some times more in a body well armed whom he finds it impractical to encounter with alone'. Later in that year the Collector put forward the idea that if parties of 'His Majesty's forces of Horse and Dragoons' could be stationed at intervals along the coast they could quickly be summoned to the aid of the Revenue men; and if they were rewarded for any captures they made it would encourage their enthusiasm.

During 1722 the incidence of smuggling increased to such a degree that many of the runs were bound to be discovered. In a typical incident during October of that year Captain Phillips, now commanding the Customs smack *Weymouth*, boarded the *Judith and Mary*, a Hull ship which had ostensibly come in from Northbergen. He and his men caught some of the crew in the very act of funnelling brandy from large barrels into smaller casks ready for distribution. All were seized and taken in triumph to the Custom warehouse.

Very often the crew of the Customs smack or the smaller boats which were used in the harbour and the backwaters were completely outnumbered by the crew of the ship that they had to board and search. This happened in November 1722, when Mr Whitcomb took his Tidesmen aboard the *Higham*, master Richard Ashby, to search for persons who might be Jacobite sympathisers. Ashby told his crew to secure the fore-scuttle which James Chapman, a Tidesman, was in the process of lifting open. Chapman's fingers were still under the scuttle when Ashby's men stamped it shut, giving him a very badly bruised hand. They also hit him over the head in the ensuing struggle, and Whitcomb decided to pull out all his men except for two who were to remain on board 'with instructions for their demeanour'. Whitcomb was pretty sure that though there were no secret agents of the Pretender on board there was a deal of contraband tucked away. History does not record how those two unfortunate Tidesmen fared or whether the contraband was discovered and the crew arrested.

The apprehension of smugglers only gave rise to further anxieties for the Collector. In 1729 he reported that he had committed to the County Gaol six men off the *Walcherin*, a   93 smuggling cutter which had become a legend on this coast. They went under a strong guard of dragoons because rumour had it that an armed ambush had been planned to effect their escape. The following January, when seven men were used to guard a band of captured smugglers who were being taken in a passenger wherry to Ipswich for a legal examination, four of the smugglers ran off as soon as the boat touched the quay and there was a mob of people gathered there to help them get away.

Often those arrested were sent by boat down the coast to the Thames and so to Newgate Prison in London. Sea transport was often easier and certainly much more secure than the highways. In 1748 two men charged with rescuing a notorious smuggler from captivity were taken from Yarmouth to Ipswich by sea for examination, and carried on from there in the Custom House smack.

Griffith Davies was Collector at Harwich from around 1730 right down to 1773 when he resigned in favour of his son. Davies was a very important man in Harwich; he was elected Mayor 15 times and was much respected in his position as Collector, and high on the ladder of Harwich society. He exacted the duty payable to the King without fear or favour and so was often in trouble with officers and crews of the packet boats. He reported to the London Commissioners that such was the sympathy of the townspeople for the smugglers, who kept them supplied with their little luxuries, that the Customs men had to run the gauntlet of their abuse as they walked about the town; if they ventured on a packet-boat their very lives were threatened. Some nasty tricks were played upon them. When Revenue boats were cut from their moorings and an anchor was stolen Davies was driven to report: 'There is a great reason to believe that the offences were committed by some malicious persons in order to render the said boats useless.'

At this time the Royal Navy was experiencing great difficulty in recruiting sufficient men for its warships. The Government found a happy solution. By far the largest number of smugglers on the east coast were experienced seamen, so their sentence when caught was to be summarily impressed into the Navy. In 1746 it was reported by the

Kirby-le-Soken. The old quay looks out on the backwaters and Horsey Island.

Harwich Custom House that 15 arrested smugglers were taken on the *Fowey* to the Nore where the Fleet was gathering, and were put aboard the *Namure*. What a relief that was is clearly recorded: 'We are glad that they are safe on board as it was with great difficulty we kept them so long. They broke through gaol twice and attempted it again yesterday but more especially as we were informed that about 60 armed smugglers were coming here with the intention to rescue them.'

When Richard Parsons was to be sent to London in January 1750 to stand trial as a smuggler, Captain Dagnett of the Harwich Revenue cutter *Walpole* had to take him, leaving the coast unguarded for some time. The Collector reported: 'we put the said Parsons on board the sloop at three o'th.clock this afternoon and the sloop sail'd soon afterwards and as the wind is likely to be fair, I believe the sloop will be up tomorrow in the evening'.

Captain Rodney, commander of His Majesty's Ship *Eagle*, was looking forward to a welcome addition to his crew when a smuggling cutter, the *Trowell and Hammer*, master Cornelius Ashpole, was caught on the Walton Backwaters by the Customs men and they sent for the armed support of the Navy. It all went wrong, though, as reported on 6 February 1746: 'Before they could get up the Handfleet Waters, the men, knowing themselves guilty, had all quitted the cutter so that the Lieutenant and [press] gang could secure none but one John Major, a sick man who was in bed in the house of Jeremiah Harris, one of the chief owners of ye said cutter, but he being one of the constables of the parish, the Lieut. would not meddle with him.'

There was an occasion when the smugglers turned the weapon of impressment back on their persecutors. A gang of them had been sailing their cutter up Woodbridge Haven when they went aground with an embarrassing amount of brandy and tea aboard. Thus they were overtaken by the Revenue cutter which seized the goods while they all made off. Naturally the master and owner of the smuggling cutter did not wish to lose his boat – he would rather turn King's evidence, have the gang indicted and get his boat back. The rest of the gang were not enthusiastic about this, and accordingly they somehow got word to the Navy to have him impressed. It worked, and the Navy arranged for him to be put on the *Boyne* at the Nore. The matter had to be taken to the highest level at the Board and the Admiralty to get the man freed as the only witness in the prosecution of the smugglers.

On 6 October 1777 the Collector at Harwich made the despairing cry for help which introduces Chapter 4. He followed it up a year later with 'a list of smuggling cutters who constantly run their goods upon the coasts of Essex, Suffolk and Norfolk':

Masters	Tons	Guns	Men
— REYNOLDS	134	12	45
Stephen CANN	75	6	24
Stephen MARSH	140	uncertain	34
John COCK	113	uncertain	28
Wm. MARSH	120	uncertain	30
James CREE	114	10	32
— BAKER	112	10	28
John GIRLAND	110	4	24

Those guns were not for decoration – they were fired in earnest in many a clash on the Essex and Suffolk coast. Back in 1726 Richard Clement, Captain of the Revenue smack *Prince of Wales*, had a report that several French ships had crept into Sizewell Bay, near Aldeburgh. The contemporary account goes on: 'he set sail, found two of them there at anchor and one of their boats on shoar and a great number of horsemen which the Captain supposes ready to receive their cargoes. As the Captain came to them there was a boat stood away from one of the French vessels, the Captain made after them upon which the Frenchman stood in again for their own vessel but the Captain cutt 'em off from boarding. Upon which both the French vessels fired upon the Captain to such a degree both their great guns and small arms that they were forced to quit them. However the Captain secured five of the men, took ten half anker casks of brandy, four rowles of chocolate and about four doz. packs of cards. The five persons above-mentioned are secured in this gaol.'

Twenty years later Captain Isaac Dagnett of the Revenue cutter *Walpole* escorted into Harwich a smuggling cutter which had only just landed its cargo on the Suffolk coast when Dagnett came up with it. He was obliged to fire at them more than once and wounded one of the smugglers before they would heave-to and surrender. 'They had sixteen stout seamen on board and for want of a Man of War's being here the Collector, as being Mayor, was obliged to put them into the gaol.' He would, of course have been pleased to get them impressed into the Navy straight away, because while they were in prison on his 'patch' they were a constant source of anxiety.

This same Captain Dagnett was out on station in the *Walpole* on a Sunday afternoon in November in 1747 when he saw a small boat a quarter of a mile off Felixstowe. He called out the boat's crew to board it, suspecting it was a smuggler. It was something more – a French privateer, the *Gilliaume Gouteux* out of Calais, worked by nine men and a boy under its master Anthony Landan. It was not much of a catch: it had no guns, just a musket and a cutlass for each man and a few pistols over. The crew were brought ashore and put in prison, but their ultimate fate is unknown.

The following February when Dagnett was ill his Mate John

The Martello tower at Clacton which today houses the Coastguard.

Wheatland took over – and had a very active day. They sighted a likely smuggler off Orford Ness and started a chase which lasted from eight in the morning until three in the afternoon. The smuggler fired repeatedly on the *Walpole* which replied in good measure, and soon both ships had their sails and rigging rent and tattered. Just as the Revenue cutter closed in to make an attempt at boarding, its topmast carried away. Cutting away the debris and getting under way took time, allowing the smugglers to beat two miles to windward, making further pursuit pointless. Nevertheless Wheatland was pleased to report that the smuggler 'received a shot between wind and watter which obliged them to keep pumping continually'.

The Revenue cutter was on the receiving end in April 1779. The *Bee*, sailing out of Harwich under the command of Captain Hart, spotted a lugger estimated at over 100 tons burthen, low in the water with what could be a heavy cargo of contraband, though she was not showing the usual smuggler's guns. The *Bee* overhauled her and prepared to send off a boarding party. Suddenly the lugger opened ports and, putting out five guns, fired constantly at the *Bee*; having the advantage of surprise, she chased the Revenue cutter through Goldiman's gap (Goldmer Gat on modern charts) into the Wallet, keeping up the cannonade. All the *Bee* could do was to get out of range as soon as possible, so she ran on up the Colne and made harbour, whereupon Hart got the fastest horse he could and rode up to Harwich 'to acquaint us that the lugger was then landing her cargo at Clacton upon this coast about eighteen miles from hence'.

Worse was to come. In October Edward Hart passed on a rumour 'from a person who is in the confidence of the smuggler upon this and the Suffolk coast' that four large well-armed cutters were about to sail in convoy and make huge landings of all kinds of contraband. They were including one Frenchman in each crew who had a special commission to act as a privateer, though the rest of them were English and Irish. This was a ploy to give them an excuse to take English ships, even Revenue cutters, as prizes. The ship they were anxious to catch was the Revenue cutter *Repulse*, for they had suffered much at Captain Harvey's hand.

It was not the *Repulse* which was captured, but the *Swift*, the smaller 47-ton cutter. The *Swift* had done well, under James Woodward's command, to stop a yawl just off the coast and had transferred from it some 25 half-ankers of brandy and geneva. But the master of the yawl was acute enough to note that the crew of the *Swift* numbered less than his own, many of whom had stayed hidden. He gave a signal and they swarmed over the side, put the crew of the *Swift* into a ship's boat and sailed away with the Revenue cutter, their own boat, and the contraband. The smugglers had the use of the *Swift* for a year until she was recognised and recaptured whilst making a smuggling foray off Hastings.

In 1778 the *Repulse* was captured – not by the smugglers but by the French. This was the third cutter of this name, and carried a crew of 42. The cutter was apparently blown ashore on the French coast, and the French were pleased to capture and imprison the crew in Calais for over a year. The crew had to pay a substantial sum to buy their release. The two mates sent a petition to the Board, asking for help to pay their fines and seeking their re-appointment. They heard that: 'As it appears to us that the said cutter was run on shore by the wilful misconduct or negligence of the crew, unconstrained by stress of weather or the superior force of the enemy, not only out of the limits of this Duty, but on a Foreign Coast, you are to acquaint them that we reject their petition, but we agree to Martin Hopkins having a new deputation to enable him to perform his duties as mate of the new *Repulse* cutter, and herewith you will receive the same.' The *Repulse* continued life as a French privateer but it was eventually recaptured by the British and returned to its owner, Captain Harvey.

In 1786 the Collector was pleased to report that more than 30,000 gallons of spirits had been seized between 10 October 1784 and 5 July 1786. There is no doubt that increasing vigilance was having an effect to the degree that in October 1795 the Harwich area could declare 'the state of smuggling upon this coast is at present at so low an ebb that we cannot hear of anything of consequence having been done in that way for a considerable time past, particularly in the last six months'.

One reason for the lull was that since 1793 England had been at war with France, yet there were still some hard battles to be fought between the Revenue men and the renegade smugglers who were ready to deal with the French. In 1807 the *Argus* Revenue cutter, cruising offshore up to Hollesley Bay just below Orford Ness, had left the Galloper light astern when, at eight o'clock at night, they sighted a suspicious-looking brig. They overhauled it but had to fire a shot across its bows before it would heave-to. The Captain of the *Argus*, John Turner, ordered a seven-man, cutlass-wielding boarding party over the side. It pulled away in the ship's boat towards the brig, the *Endeavour*, and then watched in helpless amazement as a lugger came up and engaged the *Argus* in musketry fire. The Frenchmen in the lugger appeared to get the upper hand and overwhelm the Revenue cutter's crew. The boarding party was caught between the devil and the deep. They chose the latter, boarded the brig and sailed it back to Harwich.

100

Since the *Argus* did not arrive they could only conclude that the cutter had been captured and sailed to a French port.

It turned out that the brig had already been captured by the French lugger *L'Etoile* of Boulogne. 60 tons, mounting 14 guns and with a crew of 60 it is not surprising that it was more than a match for the *Argus*, which was taken into Dunkirk. But the British had put up a fight, for five of the crew were killed and a further six including the captain were wounded. The lugger was sunk in the battle, and four of its crew went down with it, plus five prisoners the lugger had taken from the brig. Captain John Turner died of his wounds in imprisonment. Eighteen of his crew were incarcerated in French prisons, and not many survived the terrible conditions to return to England in 1815.

Places associated with smuggling in North Suffolk.

6

From the Alde to the Yare

The river Alde heads east for the sea just south of Aldeburgh, then it finds its way blocked, turns south, passes Orford and joins the Ore behind Orford Ness. From Aldeburgh the coast runs due north to Dunwich and on to Southwold. Between these two ancient boroughs – still of local importance in the 18th century, the golden age of smuggling – lay a long, lonely coastline which was eminently suited to the landing of contraband, and it was within a few miles of the main highway to Ipswich and on to London.

Above Southwold the coastline was equally lonely and well-equipped for the reception of contraband. Benacre, just inland, was a favourite smuggling centre. Further north were the great fishing ports of Lowestoft and Yarmouth. Here the trawlers and the drifters were courted for their custom by the smugglers, often Frenchmen or Dutchmen, who could sell the fishermen their contraband and leave them with the problem of getting it ashore.

Reigning over this area, the Yarmouth Collector had his hands full. Smugglers here were not averse to violence. For example, in 1709 the Yarmouth Revenue smack, under Captain Darby, stopped and boarded a suspicious-looking Dutch ship. It had 40 barrels of brandy on board and was on the way to land them. The smugglers were very annoyed: they set about the boarding party and were beating them up badly when Darby saw a boat from Gorleston within hailing distance and yelled for assistance. He was incensed that, as the Collector reported, 'they only laughed at him and would not come nigh him' – a good example of the public attitude to smuggling in those days.

A note of 'some rummaging tools . . . required for the boats' including 'one small ripping hammer and gimblets, two shovels, two rummaging lanthorns, one iron crow', put to the Board from the Colchester Collector in September 1734, gives an intriguing glimpse into one aspect of the Revenue officer's work. Down in the hold of a smuggler's ship, they would prise open panelling, test bulkheads for secret compartments, turn over loose cargoes, often filthy and suffocating, for what might lie beneath – working by the light of those flickering lanterns, and on a boat rolling and pitching to the whim of the sea. On deck above, their colleagues would stand in tense confrontation with the smuggler captain and his crew.

Hated though they were, the Revenue men were as human as the smugglers, and they had their disagreements within the service itself. In April 1771 Thomas Sherman, Inspector of the Waterguard, and John Deane, Tidesurveyor of Harwich, complained to the Board through their Collector that Mr Jackson, Surveyor of Excise at Yarmouth, would keep going to Harwich with the intention of boarding the packets and rummaging them, and the Customs men were much incensed by his interference.

But such internal dissension was as nothing compared with the dealings with the 'Free Traders'. One Excise officer was on the receiving end when, in 1729 or thereabouts, he came upon a gang of smugglers openly moving their contraband inland near Snape, some five miles from Aldeburgh. Bravely, but foolishly, he called on them to halt and they turned on him in a body. They overwhelmed him, took his sword off him and used it to cut off his nose in a gesture of defiance towards the service. When they had seen their goods well on their way they came back to kill him off and secure their anonymity, but he had managed to crawl into hiding in a thick hedge.

It had been reported that smugglers on the Suffolk coast were so well organised, so numerous and so violent that even the dragoons specially quartered along the coast to counter their operations could not equal their manpower or arms in open combat.

The strength of the smugglers in 1746 is indicated by the events that followed the arrest of 'Giffling' Jack Corbolt. Called 'Giffling', a Suffolk dialect word, because of his furious, restless nature, Corbolt was a notorious and violent smuggler with a respectable daytime profession as a Yarmouth inn-

104

keeper. The Customs officers were pleased to capture him and very determined to get him safely behind bars in the prison at Norwich Castle. Accordingly they ordered a special escort of Riding Officers to accompany him to Norwich, including Thomas Jarvis, who covered the Caister area, Robert Watson and two others, Burdett and Herring. Burdett and Watson had the prisoner with them in a chaise; Jarvis and Herring accompanied them on horseback. Everything went well until they were within six miles of Norwich, when they came up with a band of about 20 armed smugglers. Jarvis put spur to his horse and got away, but the other men were severely beaten up. 'Giffling' Jack was thus rescued and taken on to some secret hide-out in Norwich by his gleeful confederates.

These were members of the gang which, just a year before, had made several open and unopposed landings at Benacre, duly reported to London by the Yarmouth Collector: '11 July ... at 6 o'clock in the evening a gang of 50 smugglers ran a cargo of tea and brandy at Benacre Warren in Suffolk and carried it all off, armed with cutlasses and fire arms. On 25 July at 8 in the morning an armed gang of 60 smugglers landed another cargo at the same place and carried it off and about 6 o'clock that same evening another gang of 40 smugglers landed another cargo at Kesland Haven near that place and carried it all off.'

On 31 July at about eight in the morning 'upwards of 70 smugglers armed with firearms passed through Benacre Street with a large quantity of goods having with them a Brest cart laden with 4 horses. On the 1st at Night about 40 smugglers with 50 horses landed a cargo at Kesland Haven of tea and brandy in small carts and carried all off being armed with cutlasses and firearms. Without the assistance of dragoons the officers will not be able to put a stop to the pernicious practice'.

No doubt the smuggler was looked on as a 'free trader', providing a useful service to local as well as London people, offering all kinds of dutiable goods at much cheaper prices. But it was not just local popularity which caused the coastal dwellers not to co-operate with the Customs service – they were under an implicit threat to keep silent. One sentence written in 1745 succinctly describes the situation: 'A gang of smugglers on Sunday night went to the house of Helen Hurrell in ye town, broke in a window and cruelly treated one Henry Hurrell, who they apprehended had given informations against them, and afterwards put him on a horseback with only his shirt on [on a cold February night] and carried him away and he has not been heard of since.'

When the smugglers wanted to silence Samuel Dyball they had him pressed into the Navy. He served his time, was discharged in 1742 and made his way home to Gorleston. But when he went into the alehouse next door for a celebratory drink he was set upon by three salvage men known to work hand in glove with the smugglers. They beat him up so severely that 'unless he had been a strong young fellow he would in all likelihood have been killed on the spot'. Such stories would have circulated by word of mouth round the market place and far inland; fear would have kept eyes averted and mouths shut for a long time, while the gangs flourished.

The attitude of the gentry, who obtained many of their luxuries through the smuggling chain, as well as that of the ordinary folk who were often paid in kind for their assistance on the beach, was demonstrated clearly in 1718 when the Yarmouth Surveyor went to the Beccles Quarter Sessions to prosecute Coe Arnold of Lowestoft for smuggling. He reported that he found 'such a great number of local Justices of the Peace and so great a crowd of people from Lowestoft supporting Arnold, all declaring that the officers could not stop and search any man on ye road without ye assistance of a constable . . . that your Honrs. Officers were advised to withdraw ye suit'.

In March of the following year the Board made another effort to prosecute Arnold for his assault on Samuel Bayly, Surveyor at Norwich, in the course of smuggling. The case was put into the hands of 'a noted attorney'. The legality of searching him was established, the assault was proved. It was shown that Arnold ran through the White Lyon Yard in Beccles and threw his bags over a 'rail' or fence. A man called Sallows then took them away without offering or calling for help. The judge directed the jury that all was properly proved – but the jury, though sent out twice, brought in a verdict of not guilty, which, as the Collector commented, 'showed how little respect they had ... for His Majesty, His Revenue and His Officers'.

The intense atmosphere of the courtroom was a far cry from the heaving deck of a Revenue sloop, or the back of a horse on a long night's patrol, and these officers had to be versatile. Life was as hard for them as it was for the smuggler. In 1720, just before Christmas, Mr Davis the Collector at Southwold, David Lanham his deputy, William Knott and two Boatmen were coming into Southwold Haven when their boat capsized. Only William Knott was rescued: the Southwold Custom House was stripped of its senior staff at a stroke. In that same year Robert Dunn, seaman on the Yarmouth Revenue smack, was boarding a suspect fishing vessel when he was shot dead by one of the crew. Eight years later a seaman employed on a sloop in this dangerous occupation was earning just £14 a year, and glad of it.

It was in 1728 that the Yarmouth sloop, commander Captain Harrold, was on the point of boarding a smuggler when a vicious squall bore down upon it. The squall snapped the mast which fell overboard dragging four men with it, one of whom was drowned. The smugglers saw their chance and quickly made their getaway. In the following year, 1729, it was noted that 'French vessels hovering on the coast between this place and Newcastle' were selling brandy to colliers and to other local boats going about their lawful business. It is a reminder that the Revenue cutters were up against foreigners as well as Englishmen.

The English smuggling barons who lived on the Continent dealt wholesale with special distilleries set up there to serve them, and organised convoys to make landings. In December 1729 the Board was told 'There are at Calais four Merchants in company who fitt out every summer 10 snows [brig-like sailing ships with a trysail] from 40 to 60 tons. They provide the snows with good numbers of men and ammunition ... to make a vigorous defence in case they are attacked by ye officers of ye Customs ... then the distillers and other traders put in what brandy they please, some 40, some 50, some 100 casks ... then come on the coast and keep within 7 or 8 leagues one of another to be ready to assist each other in case of danger, the first that has sold his cargoes speaks with all ye

107

rest and takes from them what money they have received and goes for Calais and loads again and comes again on the coast, soe they keep a constant round of comeing with brandy and goeing with money.' Their crews operated, apparently, on the 'no purchase – no pay' principle.

The smugglers kept no records, for they would have been damning evidence if found. The Revenue officers were obliged to do so, as a Government department; they had to justify their existence, to show they earned their pay! So we are able to read the reports sent on a daily basis to London headquarters, by the Collector responsible for each area of the coast, and try to imagine the situation as it appeared to both parties from the 17th century onwards.

The constant loss of revenue through smuggling, particularly on this Suffolk coast, brought a report from the Collector at Yarmouth showing his enthusiasm for the cause as early as December 1704: 'we are really of the opinion that there ought to be a good brisk officer at Pakefield, but how it should be done with little charge we know not' – a very diplomatic letter, which goes on to recommend for such a post a Mr Robert Baker, 'who is said to be very zealous for the Queen's Service'. After the passage of so many years it would be difficult today to say whether a job was being found for the man, or a man for the job!

It is clear that someone was appointed because in 1708 the Collector wrote to his officers at Lowestoft and Pakefield mentioning that 'Our Good Friend Mr John Aldred, our Queen's Searcher, owning the Queen's Head in Lowestoft' begs them to favour his 'Publick House' for all their business with ships which 'requires to be transacted in a Publick House'. Obviously John Aldred could not be one of the many landlords who took advantage of the bargain prices offered by the 'moonshiners' as is clear from a report in 1715: 'Whereas it has been a frequent practice for French sloops to come upon the coast of Suffolk and particularly to Dunwich where they land quantities of wine and brandy so that gentlemen and Publick Houses are filled therewith (as we are told) and the officer at Southwold cannot come thither without riding seven miles about so that the Crown hath suffered much thereby – we humbly propose as a remedy thereof that a boat with two able boatmen and under the direction of a proper officer with a horse, as at Lowestoft, were fixed at Walberswick which would not only serve Southwold Haven but also Dunwich and the places adjacent.' It is interesting to note that Lowestoft was not constituted as a port until 1852, so at this time Pakefield and other little places were just as important as possible landing places for the smugglers.

One of those Calais merchants' vessels, the *Aimable*, attempting to get in touch with the colliers off Whitby, was intercepted by Captain Richard Thomas commanding H.M.S. *Hawk*, and was escorted into Yarmouth on 14 March 1731 with 344 casks of brandy in her hold. Another, the *St. John the Baptist* of Calais, was captured a fortnight later and brought in by H.M.S. *Weazel* under the command of Captain Christopher Oates. It had 200 half-ankers of brandy aboard, the equivalent of 850 gallons.

It was at this time that landings on the Suffolk coast, more particularly at Benacre, came to the attention of the Riding Officers, and it was reported on to the Board of Commissioners that 'of late here has appeared a bold and dangerous gang of smugglers between 20 and 30 in number who are well armed and hors'd ... they fear no number of officers and bid defiance to the dragoons that are quartered on the Suffolk coast. The place they have of late haunted is about Benacre. The goods they carry off are carry'd cross country to Bury and so to London'. From this report it can be seen that lines of communication for the sale of contraband were already widespread and well-arranged.

A year later in 1733 it was observed that 'considerable numbers of arm'd men appear weekly on this coast near to Lowestoft and Pakefield and carry off great quantities of tea and prohibited goods and appear in so formidable manner that your Riding Officers of the coast dare not attack them'.

The Collector was greatly exercised in his mind as to how he should deploy the limited number of men under his command to police all these lonely landing places. When he did make rearrangements they were not always popular, and the Board itself was not above making alterations against his advice. For example, Dunwich was used by the contraband runners to such an extent that the Board decided, belatedly, to switch the

Yarmouth Custom House. From here the Yarmouth Collector presided over an area of coastline rife with smugglers. (Reproduced by kind permission of H.M. Commissioners of Customs and Excise)

110

boat used by the Waterguard from Southwold to Dunwich, only to be met by the Collector's protest that 'Dunwich, whatever it might have been before, has no trade or business', whilst many more ships called at Southwold in the course of legitimate trade and needed to be cleared by the Custom House.

At the same time the Collector chivvied his local staff, reminding Mr Thornton, Riding Officer, that his specific duty was to reside at Caister and patrol regularly from Haven's Mouth to Winterton, and that he had become neglectful and must be more attentive to his duty. John Unthank, another Riding Officer, was detailed to check, very carefully, the routes which smugglers might be taking to carry their contraband towards Norwich. For this special work he was given an additional allowance of £10 a year.

Subsequently the Board asked the Yarmouth Custom House to trace the routes that smugglers on the east coast used to reach London, hoping to impose checks on contraband long after it had been landed and after the smugglers had been lulled into a false sense of security. But in those days of travel by horse on unmade roads London was a very long way off indeed; Yarmouth could only reply that they had been able to trace the gangs some 30 miles into the hinterland, but then all clues to their progress were lost. However, they passed on the information that according to hearsay the last part of the smugglers' route was through Mile End, but they varied their route and disguised their packages.

While John Unthank was faithfully performing his extra duty, another Riding Officer, one Bayfield of Mundesley, had to be dismissed because he had taken on a farm and was trying to run it alongside his work for the Revenue. Such an arrangement was specifically forbidden in his contract. Mr Thornton, the Riding Officer at Winterton, was much more attentive to Custom House business since his telling-off: 'finding some goods had been run ashore near a great meer . . . known by the name of Horsey Broad, he sent for a party of dragoons and believing the goods were concealed among the reeds in the meer he got two boats which are kept on the meer and went in search for it and, after almost 2 days and nights, he found it in a flat bottom boat hauled up on dry land amongst the reeds. There were three men with fire arms guarding it who, as soon as they saw the soldiers, threw down their arms and made their escape thro' the meer at a place where they could not pursue them with the boats'. Following such a recovery of smuggled goods Thornton would have gone up in the estimation of his Collector, and he would have been pleased to know that a report on his good work on this occasion had gone to 'head office'.

A fellow Riding Officer, John Massingham, suffered a complete reversal of fortune. In November 1744 John Cross, a smuggler of local notoriety, had been apprehended and was to be taken to court for examination and then to prison to await subsequent trial. Meanwhile he was secured in the cellar of a public house in Yarmouth market place, guarded by no less than eight dragoons. Right under their noses a servant helped him to escape through a small door to the pavement outside. There, in the presence of a great crowd of what can only be termed well-wishers, Cross was given a horse. Spurring it on he disappeared very rapidly down the street and out of town.

The Collector was incensed. He judged that Massingham, present throughout the fiasco, had been party to the escape. Even though it was possible he was threatened with injury by the smugglers to ensure his co-operation, the Collector suspended him from duty for a month without pay and ordered him to re-take Cross at his own expense in that time. If he did not do so he would be dismissed from the service.

Meanwhile arrests were being made, seizures were filling the Custom House and smugglers' boats were being confiscated, sawn up, sold off or burnt. A sale held at Yarmouth in 1730 to clear the Custom House included 'condemned' coffee, tea, geneva, rum, brandy, wine, Holland linen and calico. In 1735 the Aldeburgh Revenue smack brought into Yarmouth a cutter heavily laden with tea and brandy. On this occasion the smugglers were more submissive than aggressive. They begged that they might be allowed to sail their boat away if they transferred all the contraband to the smack with no help from the officers. Their boat was their living, when all was said and done. But the captain of the smack was adamant: 'they were deny'd', was the terse conclusion to his report.

112

It was a great day when, on 22 December 1747, two troops of dragoons numbering 160 men arrived at Yarmouth to be quartered along the coast as the Collector thought best. Some of them were in action very quickly, helping in the arrest of Samuel Wayman at his home in Yarmouth. He was considered so dangerous a threat that they put him on the Revenue smack and guarded him with six dragoons while he was taken by sea to London. As a desperate and violent smuggler Wayman would have had too many opportunities to escape if he had been taken by road through communities sympathetic to his situation.

Another smuggler captured and incarcerated in the gaol at Norwich Castle after due sentence was Stephen Rolfe. That he was a smuggler of no little education and enterprise is apparent from the letter he wrote to Mr Hoyle, the Surveyor at Norwich, and forwarded to the Yarmouth Collector who had handled his case in 1772:

'Mr Hoyle-Sir, I should be obliged to you to acquaint the Hon. Comm. I could be of infinite service should their Honours think proper to intrust me with the command of a Cutter. I could positively destroy smuggling on this coast soon. I don't meen that I can answer to take on larger Cropps than common but can and will destroy it intirely and should the Hon. Commissioners intrust me in this request you shall soon find my word true and this you may depend on.

P.S. But should their Honours distrust me, I beg of you to petition them for my being removed to London for I cannot have my health in this place nor can I be relieved from my friends. I am in the most abject distress here.

From your humble servant,
Stephen Rolfe'

The Collector's response to this singular entreaty is unrecorded.

When the dragoons had to be withdrawn because of military commitment in the War of the Austrian Succession (1740–48), the Jacobite Rebellion of 1745 and the Seven Years' War from 1756, followed later by the War of American

Independence (1775–83), the smugglers were quick to take advantage. By 1769 the Collector at Yarmouth was again asking for soldiers to be stationed in groups along the coast because the smuggling had so vastly increased, both in terms of goods landed and numbers involved. Using threats and blackmail the smugglers had all the coastal villages in thrall. By the onset of the American war the ranks of the smugglers were said to have increased threefold. In 1781, with the country hard-pressed by the mounting cost of the war in far-off America, and with the smugglers materially depriving it of a colossal sum in unpaid duty, Lord Pembroke was heard to remark 'Will Washington take America or the smugglers England first?'

Rolfe's use of the term 'Crop' refers to the cargo of contraband carried by a smuggler. It became a kind of crop to be gathered from the sea after it had been sunk with weights on to the sea bed. Its position was marked by floats whose identity was evident only to those in the know. This method was evolved in the shallows of the Essex estuaries and tidal creeks where the saltings and the marshes prevented straightforward landings. It was adopted by smugglers all along the East Anglian coast as a way of outwitting the increasing vigilance of the Waterguard men of the Customs and Excise from the beginning of the 19th century. The Maldon Collector described the method as 'sinking a string or two of tubs near the coast to be picked up by coadjutors ashore'.

To make a drop of tubs the 'tub-boat' was invented. The Harwich Collector was already being troubled by them when he reported to the Board of Commissioners in 1789 that such a boat was 'built very deep, flat floor and very full fore and aft. The timbers are small and boards thin. The thwarts are laid high, bound with iron knees to increase the stowage underneath. They have in general wash streaks upon the gunwhale which are ship'd and unship'd at pleasure. Since the Act of last session these boats have been built about a hair's breadth under the length of 18 feet and the width has been increased'. He goes on to describe 'Sinking stones' as 'bound with iron with an eye at the top for the greater security of fastening the warp rope'. To recover the goods a 'creeper' was required.

This was fashioned from iron, grapnel-like, with 'several fangs . . . used for the grappling of goods when sunk'.

A man who made a business of building such boats in Ipswich was George Bailey. He called them 'luggage boats' to disarm suspicion, but the Revenue saw through his deception. One used in 1798 was said to have a carrying capacity of up to 300 tubs. Since a tub was the same as a half-anker, which contained four and a quarter gallons, it can be seen that such a boat could sink up to 1275 gallons of spirits. It was possible to sink for later retrieval many kinds of dutiable goods, provided that they were suitably waterproofed.

In 1751 Ben Jacobs, known to the law as King of the Smugglers, was driving a cart through Ingatestone. Revenue officers were waiting for him, acting on a tip-off or on the evidence of their own patient surveillance. They arrested him, though he gave the false name of John Inglish, and searched the cart. There they found, under other goods, two tightly sealed bladders containing a total of three gallons of brandy. Such packaging could indicate that they were part of such a sinking and recovery operation. Tea, or anything else which could be successfully contained in a waterproof wrapping for a day or two on the sea-bed, was run in similar fashion.

The geneva (gin) and brandy produced at the great Schiedam distillery especially for the English market was mostly shipped through Flushing. Once the system of 'sinking' came into favour with the East Anglian smugglers the casks were provided roped together in advance. They were tied in pairs and then to a long rope. In this way the tubs, when brought ashore, could very conveniently be slung pannier-fashion across the back of a horse.

Benacre, as we have seen, was a popular spot for larger landings of the conventional type, involving large numbers of men and pack animals. Sizewell Gap was equally popular and many a tale has been handed down by word of mouth among the villagers, tales which, when compared with the prosaic language of the Collectors' reports are seen to have a very real basis in fact. For example, on 11 December 1747 the Revenue men learned of a smuggler's intention to make a considerable run. They called on the soldiers stationed nearby and

Lieutenant Dunn was ordered into action with a detachment of Royal Welch Fusiliers. The smugglers put up such a fight, however, that the Fusiliers broke off the engagement and retreated – not to their camp, but to the nearest inn, the 'Eel's Foot'.

There they were enjoying a little grog when, lo and behold, the smugglers themselves rode into the yard, some 30 of them, and all sufficiently armed and accoutred. Lieutenant Dunn was a brave man; he rallied his forces and sallied forth to challenge the smugglers who immediately opened fire and then fled in the confusion. The soldiers managed to hold on to two of the miscreants and eventually these were taken by the Revenue sloop to London, this being the surest way of preventing their rescue by their colleagues. But when all was said and done, the goods had been landed and were by then well on their way inland.

This gang was undoubtedly connected with that amorphous body known by rumour and reputation as the Hadleigh Gang. Its activities were given a gloss of respectability through popular hero-worship, even though the gang often committed violent assaults upon the Revenue men. At the peak of its activities the gang was landing enough dutiable goods to make a noticeable dent in the national income.

In 1735, having made a considerable landing of tea, the gang had moved it far inland, to one of a chain of what might be termed distributive warehouses. It was just an unremarkable, small house in the village of Semer, due west of Ipswich. But somebody in the service of the King had seen the operation; they alerted the Customs officers who, with the support of the military, broke down the door, seized the tea and stored it in the George Inn at Hadleigh for the night, under an armed guard. As it was being escorted out of town the following day the gang held up the convoy just outside Hadleigh. Their demand for its return was naturally refused, and the gang opened fire. One shot passed through the shoulder and into the chest of a dragoon and he died on the spot. Other men were wounded on both sides and three horses were killed. The gang overwhelmed the little force of soldiers and Revenue men, forced them to give up the tea and rode off with it in triumph. But that triumph was short-lived. Most of the smug-

Benacre Village. In the 1730s a dangerous gang operated here, transporting their goods to ready markets at Bury and London.

glers taking part were already known to the Customs officers and were eventually brought to trial. Two men, John Willson and John Biggs, who confessed that they had fired pistols in the fight, were sentenced to death by hanging at the very scene of their crime.

Louis Chandler, author of *Smuggling at Sizewell Gap* published in 1922 writes: 'Sizewell Gap was the most notorious place for smuggling on this coast ... It was the headquarters of the smuggling gang of the district. The Common of large extent which lay between Leiston and the Gap was as desolate as the African veldt. Vaults for storing casks of spirits were dug in the Common, the sandy soil facilitating the operation of concealment. These vaults or holes were covered with stout 117 planks, the turf was replaced, together with odd pieces of whin and gorse to divert attention. One of the smuggler's houses at Leiston had near the ridge of the roof a small wicket window, which commanded a view of the sea, and from this signals were made when a landing was desired.'

The inhabitants of Sizewell could, on occasion, see up to 100 carts gathered on the beach, and up to 300 horses which transformed the normally deserted foreshore into a representation of a horse fair. In April 1745 the Hadleigh Gang worked with two other well-known organisations from Yarmouth and Norwich to make a huge landing under armed protection of military proportions. The Revenue cutters which might have challenged them before they closed with the coast had been called away to strengthen the fleet as it faced war with France and Spain.

During this emergency the Riding Officers could still patrol but, since the military support offered by the dragoons had also been withdrawn, they could not possibly be considered a deterrent to determined, armed smugglers. Through July of that year the gang landed, with impunity, vast cargoes of contraband at Kessingland as well as at Benacre. They concentrated on 'dry' goods as opposed to the usual geneva, brandy and rum. Their routes inland allowed the luxuries beloved of Londoners to be on sale in the capital within a week, but much of their cargo could be sold locally, for Norwich was a great regional capital and the gentry were eager to patronise the price-cutting entrepreneurs who plied a profitable business in the smuggling chain.

One authority has estimated that in the last half of the year 1745 over 4,500 horse-loads of contraband were run across the beaches of Suffolk alone. This figure was probably calculated from the very interesting document preserved in the Suffolk Record Office at Ipswich headed 'An exact account of the quantity of goods smuggled into the County of Suffolk alone from 1st of May 1745 to the 1st of January 1745 [1746 by modern reckoning], being so much as came to the knowledge of the officers of the Customs and transmitted by them to the Honble. Commissioners.' It goes on to record the most amazing number of landings of contraband, many of them in broad daylight. Reading some of the entries one can get a very clear picture of smuggling on the east coast at this time.

May 8th	Forty horses loaded with Brandy and Tea landed at Sizewell.
9th	Eighty horses and upwards with dry and wet goods landed at Benacre – Cutter unknown.
17th	Thirty horses with Tea, out of one Cutter landed at Aldisburgh Sluice out of the Thunder Bolt and carried off by the Yorkshire Gang well armed.
20th	Seventy horses with dry goods landed at Sizewell out of Colbys, by the Hadleigh gang well armed.
June 5th	Thirty horses with Tea at Catcliff out of the May Flower Cutter and 36 with Brandy.
6th	Fifty horses with dry goods landed at Chapel out of the same cutter.
15th	Sixty horses and upwards with Tea landed at Benacer out of a Cutter unknown.
16th	Eighty horses mostly with Tea landed out of Colbys Cutter at Old Chapel about 2 miles from Sizewell; at the same time 54 horses all loaded with Tea landed out of the May Flower Cutter, and 20 next morning out of the same at Sizewell.
10th	Two gangs upwards of 50 each went off loaded with Tea landed at Lehole [Hollesley] out of a Dutch built Vessel.
13th	Seventy horses with dry and wet goods landed at Benacre, out of a Dutch Vessel Master unknown.
20th	Eighty horses with Tea and Wet goods landed at Leyhole out of Baldings Cutter.
22 & 23	300 half Anchors of wet goods carried off by people unknown with one cart and about 100 horses landed at Sizewell out of the May Flower Cutter.
25th	Sixty horses about 10 in the morning went off loaded with dry goods landed out of Colby's Cutter at Benacer – another gang of 40 went off in the Evening.
do.	Fifty horses and upwards with Tea and 40 with wet goods landed at Benacer out of a Dutch Vessel supposed Master John Binley.
do.	One hundred horses and upwards most loaded with dry goods out of a cutter unknown at Sizewell.
30th	Thirty six mostly with wet goods, landed out of the Thunderbolt at Kessingland.

119

August 1st   Fifty horses with Tea & Wet goods – Landed at Kessingland out of a Cutter unknown.

13th   John Pugh Riding Officer at Leiston was taken Prisoner by the Smugglers and Kept close all night and a large quantity of Goods were carried off out of a large Vessel unknown.

Sepr. 6th   Fifty horses with Tea and dry goods at Thorp.

17th   120 horses by 100 Smugglers landed out of a cutter unknown at Benacer Warren carried off by the Hadleigh Norwich and Yarmouth Gang.

25th   Eighty horses with Tea and a Cart loaded with wet goods landed near Aldborough Sluice out of a new cutter supposed to be Colby's.

October 27th   40 Horses with Tea out of a Cutter unknown – this was but a small part of her lading as there were above 100 horses along but Captain Martin [of the Revenue cutter] coming up on the coast the Cutter made off.

30th   40 horses and upwards loaded with tea landed at Dunwich out of Johnson's Cutter carried off to Saxmundham.

Novr. 10th   100 horses and upwards mostly loaded with tea the rest with wet goods landed at Sizewell out of a new Cutter which is now called Colbys.

23rd   40 horses and upwards loaded mostly with dry goods landed at Felixbury out of Johnsons Cutter carried off by Hadleigh Gang.

Decr. 11th   A cutter landed her Cargo at Sizewell which was carried off by a gang of smugglers about 50. Among which were several draft horses.

28th   100 Horses with 3 Carts went off loaded. Landed at Sizewell Mostly wet goods, and carried off by the Yorkshire Gang.

The headquarters of the Hadleigh Gang were a long 40 miles from the coast, so there is no doubt that the network of contacts and helpers had to be, and was, widespread and dependable. It was certainly still operating well in 1784 though the gang had suffered a slight reverse. They had moved a haul of 57 casks of brandy and gin across to Kettle-burgh, a small village some 13 miles inland due west from Aldeburgh, where it came to the notice of the Excise. Determined to seize it, the Excise sent a body of 12 men, well-armed to show the smugglers they meant business. All went well: they found the contraband, met with no opposition and by about four o'clock of a quiet Sunday afternoon in May they were well on the road to Woodbridge. The *Ipswich Journal* of the day takes up the story:

'. . . they were overtaken, near Easton, by a gang of villains, about 30 in number . . . who with horrid imprecations, and expressions of Murder! Murder! fell upon them in a most inhuman manner, with an intent to rescue the seizure; however the officers made a noble stand, and a bloody engagement ensued, which lasted nearly an hour, when the officers put the smugglers to flight, pursued them several miles, and maintained the seizure.

'Almost all the smugglers were wounded, and many of them desperately; five or six of the officers' party were also slightly wounded. The officers and their assistants were armed with carbines, pistols and broadswords. It is supposed that the noted George Cullum, of Brandeston, was at the head of this banditti.'

The owner of one of the horses used by the smugglers and captured by the excisemen in that action put an advertisement in the *Ipswich Journal* of 5 June:

'WHEREAS a Black Mare, about 15 Hands high, with a white mark on her nose, and one white leg behind, was on or about the 16th day of May last, taken on the road leading from EASTON toward KETTLEBOROUGH, by a party of excise officers, namely POPE, BELL, INGALL, MASON, SPELLING and CARTWRIGHT, or one of them, under pretence of her belonging to me JOHN CAGE of HAWLEY in the County of Suffolk, now I, the said John Cage, as soon as it can be discovered in whose possession the said mare is, intending to commence an action at law for the recovery thereof, do hereby offer a reward of Five Guineas to any person who will discover the person or persons detaining the said mare, and who will attend and

121

give evidence of such person having the said mare in his possession, on the trial of such action.
HAWLEY, JUNE 5, 1784.

JOHN CAGE'

One might be forgiven for assuming that Cage was attempting to quell the suspicion that he might be a member of the gang, but the Excise officers were more than equal to this ploy. They inserted their own advertisement, dated 23 June 1784:

'WHEREAS, JOHN CAGE, of Haughley, in the county of Suffolk, did, on the 5th inst., advertise a reward of Five Guineas to any person who would discover in whose custody a black mare was, which he insinuates to be his property, and said to be taken, under a pretence of belonging to a gang of smugglers, near Easton, in this county, on 16th May last:
NOW THIS IS TO INFORM the said Cage, That a black mare taken that day is in the possession of Mr. Geo. W. Cartwright, of the Excise office, London, and if he, the said Cage, or any of his vile associates, will discover who it was that rode the said mare at the time, or any more . . . of that gang of banditti, who attempted to murder the revenue officers, and to rescue the run goods then seized in their possession, he or they shall, on conviction of such persons, receive the sum of One Hundred Pounds, to be paid by us.'

Edward Fitzgerald (1809–83), the English scholar and poet who was born in Suffolk, wrote to his friend Charles Keene, the book illustrator: 'I have, like you, always have, and from a child have had, a mysterious feeling about the 'Sizewell Gap'. There were reports of kegs of Hollands found under the Altar Cloth of Theberton Church nearby, and we children looked with awe on the 'Revenue Cutters' which passed Aldbro', especially remembering one that went down with all hands, the Ranger.' This is clear evidence of the smuggling on this coast continuing well into the 19th century. Fitzgerald's mention of Theberton church being used to hide contraband is an echo of the indictment of John Harvey for smuggling more

122

than 50 years before, on 22 June 1747. The indictment declares that he, 'together with a number of 80 persons, on the 30th June, 1746, in the parish of Sheverton, [Theberton] there carrying firearms and other offensive weapons in order to commit the clandestine running of certain uncustomed goods, to wit: About 50 hundred weight of Tea from parts beyond the sea from which goods were customs due to His Majesty'.

This John Harvey, of Pond Hall near Hadleigh, was one of the leaders of the Hadleigh Gang. His name was one of those published in the *London Gazette* as a known smuggler, who was to surrender to the authorities or face transportation when he was apprehended. He was brought for trial partly on that account and partly on account of the Theberton escapade. A witness testified that Harvey was there, armed with a brace of pistols; that he helped to run tea and brandy ashore and that he took his own share of both. A second witness corroborated the evidence, Harvey was found guilty and sentenced to seven years' transportation.

Leonard P. Thompson tells a wonderful story in *Smugglers of the Suffolk Coast* which, in less detail, found its way into the *Ipswich Journal* of 27 June 1778. A gang at least as well-organised as the Hadleigh Gang landed some 300 casks of gin at Sizewell, enough to need six carts to carry it inland. It was safely moved to a barn on Leiston Common Farm some two miles away under the care of Crocky Fellowes, a farm worker whose master winked at such arrangements as long as he received the odd cask.

It was Clumpy Bowles, the breeches maker in Leiston who spotted the unusual activity and told Read the Riding Officer. Read, after some difficulty, found support from fellow officers and some dragoons and proceeded to the barn. Here Fellowes and two of his confederates, Sam Newson of Middleton and 'Quids' Thornton the miller, having been forewarned, staged a short diversion, arguing with the preventive men while a score of their mates moved the casks. They were moved up a ladder into the barn loft, across it and down another ladder to the other end of the building – which was partitioned on the ground floor – and so into wagons which had been brought up on this side of the barn, which happily abutted onto the lane. They locked that side of the barn as Crocky Fellowes opened

123

up the other end to the preventive officers; as soon as they were in he locked it again and slipped away. The wagons rolled on to Coldfair Green where, at dead of night, the casks were unloaded into a vault, the trapdoor to which was hidden under a huge midden. There were tea and tobacco already stored there, but room was made for the casks and the stinking midden was shovelled back over the trapdoor.

This had provided a lot of extra work and worry for the gang, and it did not take them long to find out who had split on them. In due course they called on Clumpy Bowles, so-called because he had a club foot, at his cottage on the Yoxford Road just out of Leiston. They took him, gagged him with his own neckerchief tied round the bung of a beer barrel, and flogged him unmercifully with their whips, all the way from Leiston through Friston, Snape, Dunningworth and Blaxhall – making him stagger more than five miles under continual assault. When he collapsed, apparently dead, they threw his body into a hedge to delay discovery.

But he was found next morning by a labourer, and he was still alive and ready to talk. After they had taken him to the Green Man at Tunstall and heard his story, a girl there recognised the bung used to gag him: she had marked it specially when she had lent it to Tom Tibbenham, and Clumpy said he was there at the flogging, along with Nosey Debney. They were rounded up that very day, taken off to prison at Woodbridge and eventually imprisoned at Ipswich for two years.

The story does not end there. The contraband was still stored in the vault, and the smugglers had remained tight-lipped about its location. There came the day when they thought it safe to open it up and move the goods on. They shovelled their way to the trapdoor and opened it up, and two of their number, William Cooper and Nosey Debney's brother Robert, clambered down in. They did not come out again alive. Black George Nicols bravely went down after them but had to be dragged back, quite overcome by the toxic fumes which had collected beneath the midden. Fear now made the smugglers sweat more than they had with the effort of hiding the casks. They cleared away the midden, broke in the roof of the vault and found their comrades dead.

Now they had to move the contraband on with the greatest possible haste, for the deaths could not be kept secret. Mr Ingall, the Excise officer at Saxmundham (the man who signed the advertisement for Cage's horse), soon heard of the fatalities, but he had to guess where the smugglers had headed with their albatross of a hoard. He knew the Parrot and Punchbowl at Aldringham was a favourite haunt of smugglers, and on a hunch he went there with two dragoons for company. He was right: there were the wagons, the contraband and the smugglers who, quite overcome with shock and physical effort, allowed themselves to be arrested without a struggle.

All that is left today to mark these events which so disturbed several villages in Suffolk in that summer of 1778 is a copy of the eroded inscription on the tombstone of those two unfortunate men:

Robert Debney and William Cooper
Died 22 June 1778
R.D. aged 28 and W.C. aged 18

All you dear friends that look upon this stone
Oh! think how quickly both their lives were gone;
Neither age nor sickness brought them to decay
Death quickly took their strength and sense away
Both in the prime of life they lost their breath,
And on a sudden were cast down by death,
A cruel death that could no longer spare
A loving husband, nor a child most dear,
The loss is great to those they left behind,
But they thro' Christ 'tis hoped true joy will find.

It was not long before the smugglers forgot this salutary example, for on 4 August 1810 the *Suffolk Chronicle* records: 'On the 28th ult. the Sitter and Boatmen belonging to the Customs of Southwold, seized an open Lugger, on Sizewell Beach, with 187 half ankers of Geneva on Board. And on the 29th ult. Messrs. J. Easey and R. Gildersleeves, riding officers, seized 42 half ankers of Geneva, which they found concealed in a vault in a barnyard, in the parish of Leiston.'

While the officers ashore were playing their part in filling

125

Fishermen in their shod at Pakefield, which was a shelter made from an upturned boat sawn in half.

the Custom House with seized contraband the Revenue cutters were even more uncomfortably at work off the coast. Let us take for example the *Ranger*, operating out of Yarmouth from 1813. In 1817, late in the evening of Wednesday 19 March, she came up with the smuggling lugger *Folkestone*, equipped with a crew of 36 and a threatening array of 11 carriage guns. The traditional warning shot fired across her bows to make her heave-to was not only ignored but returned in good measure. Stuart Brown, writing in the *East Anglian Magazine* of October 1953, continues the story:

'A fierce and bloody fight ensued which lasted for an hour and a half. At length, despite her inferior armament, the "Ranger", by accurate gunfire gained the upper hand and the lugger's crew launched their boats, abandoned ship and made their escape in the darkness. The lugger had received severe

126

damage from the "Ranger's" broadsides and two dead smugglers were left on board. The "Ranger" herself had three of her crew killed and seven wounded, four with severe injuries.'

He goes on to say that the dead men on the cutter were taken into the Wrestlers Inn at Yarmouth and from there they were taken to the church in a solemn procession with the Collector William Palgrave and the Comptroller John Preston leading the crew and the rest of the Custom House officers and men. The Revenue cutter *Tartar* fired a salute and men from its crew carried the coffins.

The two dead men from the lugger were given an ignominious burial in the same churchyard at the instigation of the Parish Overseers. Their lugger was brought into Yarmouth by the *Ranger*, and eventually cargo and boat together were valued at no less than £10,000 – which in the money of the day was a quite phenomenal sum. Captain Sayers and his crew were specially thanked by the Lords of the Treasury, this being an important seizure. It included no less than 1452 casks of different sizes of brandy and other spirits, plus bales of tobacco, bales of silk, bags of tea and boxes of playing cards.

One of the saddest tales to be told in the long history of confrontation between 'free traders' and Revenue men was due to forces far beyond the puny strength of man; since it concerned the *Ranger* it is a suitable note on which to end this chapter.

The *Ipswich Journal* reported the terrible storm on the night of 13 October 1822:

'This coast was visited on Sunday night last with a most dreadful gale of wind from the N.E., which came on very suddenly about half-past-ten o'clock. On the abatement of the gale it was ascertained that an immense deal of damage had been done to the shipping along the coast to the northward of this place.

'The beach for many miles was literally covered with pieces of wreck, and from the bodies washed on shore no doubt remained but that several vessels had been wrecked on the beach, with the loss of all hands.

'About 30 sail cut from their anchors in our roads, and during Monday many were seen running through for shelter, and others in a very distressed state. In the course of the morning of Monday, an alarming report was very prevalent in this town of the loss of the Ranger Revenue cutter, Capt. John Sayers, belonging to this station, and as the day advanced, it became more general.

'The anxiety and fears of the wives and relations of those on board, on hearing of this rumour, were truly distressing; they were running about with tears in their eyes, in the greatest despair, seeking for information, but nothing satisfactory could be learnt.

'In the evening, however, all doubts on the subject were entirely removed, and certain intelligence was brought of her being lost, with all on board, off Hasborough during the gale of the previous night. Her crew consisted of 38 persons, including Captain John Sayers, and Mr. Ballard, the First Mate. Of these, 8 survive, 7 of whom were in a boat upon the look out for an expected smuggler, but the gale coming on they fortunately put into Cromer, and thus escaped the fate of their unfortunate messmates.

'There was another boat out belonging to the Ranger upon the same service, which however, is supposed to have reached the cutter and got on board, or was upset at sea, as the boat was washed on shore the following morning. The eighth surviving man was sick on shore at this place . . . As every soul on board was drowned, amounting to 30, no certain information can, of course, be obtained of the exact manner in which this melancholy affair occurred. The wreck of the cutter washed on shore the following morning, as did also the body of Mr. Ballard, the first mate, and several others of the crew have since been picked up, but we are sorry to state that that of her lamented commander has not yet been found.

'The melancholy tidings of the loss of the Ranger and her crew were communicated to the relatives of Capt. Sayers as soon as prudence would dictate, and we need not picture to our readers the agonizing and distressing state of his family since . . . The service loses in him a most indefatigable and efficient commander.'

Despite this very sympathetic report it would appear that there was a lingering antipathy to the tax-collecting activities of the Revenue. In the *Norfolk Chronicle* a Mr Wheatley of Mundesley claimed that Happisburgh people 'shamefully neglected the signals of distress made by the Ranger. The shrieks of the crew were heard distinctly on the shore, yet no attempt was made to rescue.' Though this was denied by another correspondent from Happisburgh, it was noticed that local people did not come forward to express their regret wholeheartedly.

For all the quiet heroism of the crews of the Revenue cutters, against natural hazards and in hand-to-hand encounters with the violent men of the smuggling fraternity, the *Victoria History of the County of Suffolk* is not enthusiastic about the system or its efficacy: 'The Suffolk coast was a favourite one on which to run cargoes, for it offered facilities in landing absent in Essex while it was little further from the continental ports. The institution of revenue sloops about 1698 was not of much avail, if only because the Customs Commissioners and the Admiralty disputed as to which body was to provide them, and the latter department had quite enough on its hands without having to protect the revenue.'

It makes an eye-opening assessment of the smugglers' ships of the 18th century, 'built for speed and well armed', and running with 'almost the regularity of a cargo liner of today [1907]'. Such craft, often specially built on the Channel coast of the Continent, displaced up to 200 tons and were perfectly capable of taking on the armed might of a Naval cutter, not to mention a Revenue smack. The *History* suggests that a certain amount of collusion was involved in some of these encounters: 'Many of the customs officers were amenable to threats; more still had their price', and 'By law a captured smuggling vessel should be burnt, therefore when taken at sea it was more profitable to the captors to remove the cargo and receive a gratuity to let the vessel escape. Later yet, the law made it more advantageous to the revenue officers to take only part of the cargo and save themselves the trouble and risk of prosecution which had to be carried on at their own expense.' Such prosecutions could easily fail when the jury was in sympathy with the smugglers, or when they feared the threats of such men who, after all, lived in their own locality. The injury or murder of a Customs man did not warrant as much outrage as an attack on a fellow townsman.

So smuggling along the Suffolk coast continued right   129

through to the end of the Napoleonic war. After 1815 the Government had more men and resources at their disposal, and the time to turn their attention to the stopping-up of this great drain on the national income. The coast blockade system as introduced into Kent and Sussex was here modified to make use of the Martello towers, built at great expense to resist a possible French invasion. An integrated look-out system now foiled those large landings. With the formation of the Coast-guard service in 1829, first under Customs control, then passing to the Admiralty in 1831, the flood of contraband became a trickle and the stories of the old days of sea and spirits and blood and thunder passed into the folklore of East Anglia.

7

From the Yare to Stiffkey

From Caister the crumbling cliffs and sand dunes of the low-lying Norfolk coastline curve north-west towards the Wash, interrupted at intervals by cart gaps which give access to the foreshore. All along the coast the wind and sea fret at the shoreline, grinding it to fine sand which is carried away on the currents and deposited as treacherous offshore sandbanks. Happisburgh churchyard has been the final landfall of many sailors, shipwrecked on the sands where Happisburgh light now blinks a solemn warning. The once-remote fishing villages have blossomed as holiday resorts or industrial centres such as the natural gas terminal at Bacton, and the lonely beaches of the 18th century which gave such opportunities for smugglers are now hard to visualise – except perhaps on a day of winter solitude, under a huge dark sky, with a freezing east wind blowing in off the North Sea.

Just inland, North Walsham was at the time of our story a thriving market town and smuggling centre. Linked by a network of roads to the villages in those gaps where the packhorses came straight off the beach, North Walsham also had direct access south to Norwich, and west through Norfolk to the Bedford Levels and on to Peterborough, Northampton-shire and all the roads which run south-west to London.

From the Yare round to the estuary of the little Stiffkey Brook just west of Blakeney there were dozens of places where contraband could be taken ashore. The sea journey from the Continental ports was further but the profits were still good enough to justify the range and the risk. At places like Blakeney and Cley the tide left wide acres of shore exposed, and a favourite practice of smugglers was to beach their boats far out on the glistening sands to meet the labourers who gathered seaweed for strewing over the fields. The contraband

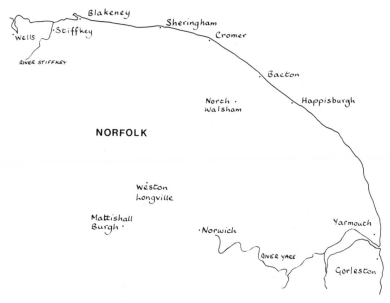

Places associated with smuggling in North East Norfolk.

could be stowed under the loads in their carts – and to the watcher on shore the participants in the drama were the merest specks against the vast backdrop of a grey Norfolk sky.

A lady interviewed in the 1920s told of a journey taken in a horse and trap with her aunt from Weybourne through the country lanes to Norwich. She was very old when she told her tale, and the period of which she spoke must have been the middle of the last century. The day was fine and the horse clipped along merrily until a man stepped out from the hedgerow, stopped the trap, told the aunt and the little girl not to get excited and led the horse through a gate and into a field on the other side of the hedge. 'Don't move or even look till I come back', he said, 'The young lady must keep her eyes shut, or it will be the worse for her.' Of course, being a child with a child's curiosity, she peeped through the hedge and saw, through the greenery, a procession of men leading horses loaded pannier-style with a barrel on each side. They passed furtively; silence returned; and after an interval the man came back, led the pony and trap into the road and apologised for the delay. The notes of this unusual encounter can still be read in the Essex Record Office.

Charles Harper, writing in 1909, tells an amusing tale of smuggling at Blakeney: 'This coast is rich in what are known as cart "gaps" – dips in the low cliffs, where horses and carts may readily gain access to the sea. These places were, of course, especially well watched by the preventive men, who often made a rich haul out of the innocent-looking farm carts, laden with seaweed for manure, that were often to be observed being driven landwards at untimely hours of night and early morn. Beneath the seaweed were, of course, numerous kegs. Sometimes the preventive men confiscated horses and carts, as well as their loads, and all were put up for sale. On one of these painful occasions the local custom-house officer, who knew a great deal more of the sea and its ways than he did of horses, was completely taken in by a farmer-confederate of the smugglers whose horses had been seized. The farmer went to make an offer for the animals, and was taken to see them. The season of the year was the spring, when, as the poet observes, "a young man's fancy lightly turns to thoughts of love" – and when horses shed their coats. Up went the farmer to the nearest horse, and easily, of course, pulled out a handful of hair. "Why", said he in the East Anglian way, "th' poor brute hev gotten t' mange, and all tudderuns 'ull ketch it, ef yow baint keerful." And then he examined "tudderuns", and behold! each *had* caught it: and so he bought the lot for five pounds. That same night every horse was back in its own stable.'

The Yarmouth cutters ranged all the way up this coast in search of smugglers, and not without success. The aptly named *Hunter* carried 14 guns and a crew of 32. In June 1784 she was well up off the Norfolk coast when she spotted something going on across the sands of Sea Palling. By the time a boat's crew had been ordered over the side and pulled ashore there was no sign of man or beast, but there were 174 half-ankers of geneva left right there on the beach.

Just two months later, in August, that same boat's crew had a terrifying experience. The *Hunter* was cruising off the same area of coast when a lugger hove into view. It appeared from

133

Blakeney, where seaweed carts brought back contraband picked up from smugglers far out on the sandbanks.

'the cut of its jib' to be a smuggler. The Revenue cutter lowered a boat manned by 12 men under the command of the second mate, and the boat approached the lugger with the intention of boarding it and making a search. Their suspicions were confirmed when the smugglers opened fire, but the second mate persisted and came alongside. He called on the captain of the lugger to surrender. The smuggler's answer was to raise a blunderbuss and shoot one of the crew dead. In a further exchange of fire another Revenue man was wounded. The smugglers then loaded one of their cannon with any bits and pieces of metal that lay to hand, including an axe, and fired it at the boat. Understandably, following the shock of the gun's report and the awesome rush of the projectiles – which thankfully missed their target – the boat's crew broke off the action and the smugglers made their escape. The outcome of that particular engagement has unfortunately been lost – one of the many gaps which time has made in the old records.

In July 1793 the *Hunter* had another violent encounter with a smuggling lugger which fought so vigorously that two of the

Revenue men were very seriously injured. From the area of engagement in Southwold Bay the men were taken as quickly as wind in sail would allow to Southwold, where they were lodged in the Old Swan Inn, still in business today as the Swan Hotel. But despite being given all medical attention both men died within a few days.

Yet that tragedy was as nothing when compared to the dreadful events of 18 February 1807, when a storm which reached a horrific crescendo at three in the morning caught the *Hunter* out on its routine patrol. The ship was overwhelmed, capsized and lost. The bodies of the crew were recovered in ones and twos as they were washed ashore; there were no survivors.

A tribute to cutters like the *Ranger* and the *Hunter* and their crews was penned by Captain Marryat, the naval officer and novelist, who around 1823 was commanding just such a cutter to assist the Revenue in the Channel patrol. Marryat wrote *Mr. Midshipman Easy*, *Masterman Ready* and other adventure stories, including *The Three Cutters* (1836) before he left the Navy and settled on a farm at Langham in Norfolk in 1843. He had a very personal knowledge of Revenue ships and men, and in *The Three Cutters* he described just such a ship:

'She is a cutter; and you may know that she belongs to the Preventive Service by the number of gigs and galleys which she has hoisted up all around her. [These were the boats used by boarding and shore parties in the pursuit of smugglers.] She looks like a vessel that was about to sail with a cargo of boats. Two on deck, one astern, one on each side of her. You observe that she is painted black, and all her boats are white. She is not such an elegant vessel as the yacht [which he had previously described] and she is much more lumbered up. She has no haunches of venison over the stern; but I think there is a leg of mutton, and some cabbages hanging by their stalks. But revenue cutters are not yachts. – You will find no turtle or champagne; but, nevertheless, you will, perhaps, find a joint to carve at, a good glass of grog, and a hearty welcome.

'Let us go on board. – You observe the guns are iron, and painted black, and her bulwarks are painted red: it is not a very becoming colour; but then it lasts a long while, and the dockyard is not very generous on the score of paint – or

135

lieutenants of the navy troubled with much spare cash. She has plenty of men and fine men they are; all dressed in red flannel shirts, and blue trousers; some of them have not taken off their canvass or tarpauling petticoats, which are very useful to them, as they are in the boats night and day in all weathers.'

Smuggling can be seen from a point of view other than that of the two protagonists. The willing customer encouraged the trade, but very few of the people who took advantage of the smuggler's offer ever admitted it in cold print. Parson James Woodforde of Weston Longville did not do that exactly: he merely committed the facts to his diary – and that diary stayed unread by the public at large until it was edited, printed and published in five volumes between 1926 and 1931. Though the references to smuggling are few, they are illuminating regarding the attitude of ordinary people of the time to the imposition of taxes on so many of their little luxuries.

Parson Woodforde's diary provides us with a vivid picture of country life in the age of smuggling in a small village deep in rural Norfolk, yet only ten miles from Norwich. James Woodforde was born in 1740 at Ansford in Somerset where his father was Rector, as well as being Vicar of Castle Cary. James went to Winchester and Oxford, and for ten years from 1763 he served as a Curate in Somerset parishes, learning his father's profession. In 1774 he was presented by New College, of which he was a Fellow, to the living at Weston Longville.

He was nearly 36 when he set up house there, as a bachelor who would need help. On 3 June 1740 he confided to his diary: 'Two servant maids came to me this morning and offered their services to me. I agreed with them both.' So he formed his household, which included a strong young man who helped him farm the land that went with the parsonage. By 14 September of that first year he could write: 'Very busy all day with my Barley.' Though he had to call in hired help to harvest his crop he was to be found working alongside them. It was Macaulay who wrote of just such a country parson that 'often it was only by toiling on his glebe, by feeding swine, and by loading dung carts, that he could obtain daily bread'.

On 3 June 1776 he hired an 'upper servant' at £5.5s.0d. a year, 'and tea twice a day'. Since tea was a very heavily taxed

136

item such a clause in the contract was an important consideration. Another servant maid who was to do the milking 'etc.' was to be paid £3.10s.0d. a year. Next day he gave the man 'who draws teeth in this parish, 2s.6d. to pull a tooth which had pained him all night. Given a steady demand in the village, the tooth-drawer would have been able to live in some comfort. Wages of workmen can be judged from his employment of two masons, a carpenter and two labourers for one week, which cost him just £2.12s.10½d. Benjamin Legate, an experienced farm labourer who did all the important work with animals and agriculture for the parson, received £10 a year. But Woodforde was not a hard employer; he paid the going rate and employed the servants expected of him in his station in village life. One entry shows his interest in those who worked for him, or rather with him: '1776 Dec 10th . . . Mr. Chambers the Schoolmaster, who is lately come here called on me to let me know that he would teach my servants Ben and Will to write and read at 4s.6d. a quarter each.' Such expense should be set against the entry for 29 March 1777: 'Andrews the Smuggler brought me this night about 11 o'clock a bagg of Hyson Tea 6 Pd. weight. He frightened us a little by whistling under the Parlour window just as we were going to bed. I gave him some Geneva and paid him for the tea at 10/6 per Pd.' It was probably Andrews who had obtained the geneva or gin, for on 27 May 1780 we find Woodforde keeping the following account in his diary: 'To Richd. Andrews for 2 Tubbs of Ginn pd. 2.10.0.' That this was the going price is confirmed by another entry in October two years later: 'To Clark Hewitt this Evening for a Tub of Gin wch. he brought in a Basket, smuggled Gin pd. 1.5.0.'

In the following November he records that 'Clerk Hewitt of Mattishall Burgh brought me a Tub of smuggled Gin about 4 gallons; just as we were at Dinner today – for which I paid him 1.5.0. Gave him besides for bringing it to me 0.1.0. He stayed and had dinner with our Folks in the Kitchen.' This shows how the smuggler was readily accepted in the houses even of men of the cloth and enjoyed their hospitality, dining on equal terms with the servants and not being thought any the less of for being a smuggler. The trade was so well organised that Woodforde could write on 12 June 1783: 'Clerk

Mattishall, where Clerk Hewitt the smuggler lived. He and his friends kept Parson Woodforde supplied with smuggled gin and brandy.

Hewitt of Mattishall brought me this Afternoon a Tub of Gin – And as my last was deficient 2 or 3 Bottles of Measure – was allowed 3/0d – therefore I only paid for the above 1.2.0. Gave Clerk Hewitt for his trouble of bringing it 0.1.0.'

That secrecy was very necessary in the disposal of contraband is shown by the entry of 29 December 1786: 'Had another Tub of Gin and another of the best Coniac Brandy brought me this Evening abt. 9. We heard a thump at the front door about that time, but did not know what it was, till I went out and found the 2 Tubs – but nobody there.'

Woodforde had more than one connection which enabled him to obtain his spirits at a bargain price. A regular supplier was Robert Buck, village blacksmith of Honingham, three miles south of Weston. We can imagine Parson Woodforde on a fine day in June 1788 'Very busy this morning in bottling two Tubbs of Gin and one of Coniac Brandy this Morn' which came in the night from Bucks from Honingham.' It is rather amusing to read just how much he used Buck in his proper capacity as a blacksmith as compared with his dealings in contraband. For example, just four days after the above entry he entered: 'To my Man Ben for things pd. 4.4.8. that is, £1.18s.0d. for a tub of Coniac Brandy of four gallons by Moonshine Buck and £2.6s.0d. for two Tubbs of Geneva of 4 gallons each by ditto and the odd 8d. for Horses Shoes removed.' Even the parson acknowledged the nickname 'Moonshine' by which Buck must have been known over a wide area around his village. Five years later, on 7 March 1794, the parson reports: 'Had 2 Tubbs of Geneva brought me this evening by Moonshine, 4 gallons each Tub.' The very next day he was 'Busy this morning in bottling off Moonshine', so we see the word used to mean contraband spirit itself. The parson always seemed to do his bottling early of a morning. No doubt he felt it wise to get rid of the tubs as soon as possible, for they could be considered solid evidence of criminal dealing. He also thought it best not to be seen messing about with spirits, funnels and bottles by any chance visitor during the day. There was a risk, for he notes: '1784. Feb. 16. Mr. Matthews, Exciseman of Mattishall, with whom Mrs. Davy boards, called here about noon.' He would have been glad on that day that he had done his bottling at first light.

James Woodforde's diary continues up to 1802 and he died on 1 January 1803, but the last entry mentioning the delivery of smuggled spirits occurs in 1794. It may be that the French wars had by then reduced the supply of gin and brandy to the Norfolk coast, or it could have been the increased vigilance of the Navy and the Revenue which frightened off the smugglers. On 16 February 1798 Woodforde writes wistfully: 'Paid John Reeve [landlord of the Heart, Weston Longville] for 2 doz. of Port Wine 3.6.0. 13 Quart Bottles to the Dozen – an amazing price indeed, 33s.0d. per Dozen. In the Year 1774 we had Port Wine at New-College at 1s.6d. per Qt. Bottle.'

Parson Woodforde was ready to accept smuggling as an economic necessity, but there were other clergymen who were prepared to work even more closely with the smugglers. In the early years of the 19th century the new young Rector of Wadham-cum-Palling, the Reverend Ready, was advised by the old man he was replacing that he should leave his barn door open at night and look on his doorstep first thing each morning. If he saw a tub of brandy or gin there he was to take

139

it in at once, and then make sure that no-one went into the barn from that day until he saw another tub outside his door. That was the token of thanks from the smuggler, who used the barn to hide a large load of contraband until it could be distributed in smaller lots. The truth of this story is vouched for by Oliver G. Ready, son of the new young parson, in *Life and Sport on the Norfolk Broads*, published in 1910. A glance at the map shows how convenient such an arrangement could have been. The cart gap north of the Marcom Hills on the coast allowed loaded carts to pass from the beach to the village of Sea Palling; the contraband could then be taken by road to Stalham, to join the highway to Norwich and the world at large.

In *Smugglers of the Suffolk Coast* Leonard Thompson makes another point: 'The Norfolk coast, perhaps to an even greater extent than that of Suffolk, afforded many ideal locations for the landing of contraband. Once clear of beach and marshland, distribution all over the county was carried out with ease and in comparative safety by transporting goods in boats along rivers and over broads. The Reverend Ready's barn, therefore, was in frequent request, not only because it was above suspicion, but also because it was conveniently near Hickling Broad.'

W. A. Dutt, whose book *The Norfolk and Suffolk Coast* was published in 1909, reproduced a number of tales told by people who could speak of their fathers being employed in smuggling, preventing smuggling, or simply taking advantage of the low prices the smugglers charged for their goods. One old inhabitant told him of the situation obtaining at Blakeney when the news was noised abroad that a ship was coming in at night to unload its contraband. The old fellow lived at Edgefield, and he claimed that every man there who owned or had the use of a horse and cart would take it down to the harbour to wait on the likely landing. For that service he would receive two shillings and sixpence. When the boat could creep in safely, enabling the carts to load and take away its cargo to safe storage, every man who had helped in this manner was paid five shillings. Five shillings on one night was a lot for a farm worker who received only ten pounds in a whole year from his employer. The teller of this story is recorded as concluding 'When we'd gone you could hear the guns of the Preventive men; but they never caught us, because they knew where we had left them a keg. And we always left a keg just inside the parson's gate.' Yet another clerical connection?

When the Reverend Francis Cunningham of Lowestoft became involved in smuggling it was as the innocent tool of a very plausible rogue. He answered a knock on the door and found a sailor standing there who entreated him to give the last rites to a shipmate who was at death's door on a ship in the harbour. The vicar compassionately agreed to go with the man, boarded the ship and found the sick sailor speechless and almost lifeless in his bunk. The rites were performed and he was conducted over the side again. So sure was the master that the man would die in the night that he arranged the burial ashore the next morning with the Rector, asking him to conduct the service. The master explained the urgency by saying that he hoped to catch the next tide while the wind was favourable. The sexton was hauled out of bed early to dig the grave and at the appointed hour the corpse was brought to the church in a decent coffin by his sorrowing messmates. The following day the worthy Rector was astonished to hear that during the night the grave had been violated, the coffin dug up and carried away. Much later he learned not only that the seaman he had visited was still in the land of the living and in rude health, but also that the corpse over which he had so sadly read the burial service was a large consignment of valuable lace which was soon on sale in the high-class London shops. The ship meanwhile had left harbour with all possible speed.

There was one man of the day who had a good word for parsons, by exception if not by recommendation. When Lord Orford's Norfolk regiment was helping to guard the coast in co-operation with the Riding Officers and the Revenue cutters in 1778 and 1779 they had quite a few clashes with the 'Free Traders', including a 40-mile chase inland from Dunwich. After such experiences Lord Orford was heard to remark that every man in Aldeburgh was a smuggler except the parson. That there were men of the cloth who were prepared to stand up and be counted as being totally opposed to smuggling is further supported by the publication, by the Reverend Robert Hardy, of his *Serious Cautions and Advice to All Concerned in Smuggling* in 1818. He defined smugglers in three classes:

'1. Those who employ their capital in the trade.
2. Those who do the work.
3. Those who deal in Smuggled Articles, either as Sellers or Buyers.'

He stated that all three groups were involved in the *guilt* of such unlawful traffic, but its *moral injuries* were suffered chiefly by the second group. He goes on to say 'Smuggling has not been confined to the lower orders of people, but from what I have heard, I apprehend that it has very generally been encouraged by their superiors, for whom no manner of excuse, that I know of, can be offered. I was once asked by an inhabitant of a village near the sea whether I thought there was any harm in smuggling. Upon my replying that I not only thought there was a *great deal of harm* in it, but a *great deal of sin*, he exclaimed: "Then the Lord have mercy upon the county of Sussex, for who is there that has not had a tub?" '

And what trouble a 'tub' could sometimes cause! Old John Buck of East Tuddenham who died at the end of 1928, aged 80, could tell a tale of his grandfather – that same 'Moonshine' Buck who kept Parson Woodforde supplied. On one occasion he had a tub of gin and some envious person reported it to the Customs. Someone told him they were on their way, so 'Moonshine' got out his cart and hurried the cask off to Frans Green, a couple of miles away up a country lane. There he got his mate, Billy Atterton, to let him put it under the bed where Billy and his wife were in bed suffering from suspected small-pox. 'Moonshine' got back in time to be relaxed and co-operative when the Preventive men arrived. They dragged the ditches and dug up the garden, but they could not find the gin and had to go away empty-handed. When all the excitement was over Buck went back for his gin, but as his grandson put it, 'Billy and his wife had necked the lot.' As related in Chapter One, Buck was caught with a tub in his house in the summer of 1792 and was very fortunate to escape with a fine, for he could have spent a very unpleasant time in Norwich prison.

142

That prison held many a smuggler but one man it could not hold was John Pixley. He was a real turncoat, for he had been a Customs officer until he decided that there was more to be made out of contraband. He swims into our view out of the records of the Thetford Assizes where, in 1740, he was found guilty of armed smuggling and sentenced to transportation to the colonies, for 'feloniously assembling and riding with three or four more persons with fire-arms in order to be aiding and assisting the clandestine running of goods.' Before he could be sent down to London and the convict ship he escaped. Recaptured the following year, he escaped again, even though under a military escort, and got clear away to the Continent. There he joined the coterie of English smugglers who lived at Flushing and bought their brandy and their gin from the Schiedam distilleries by the shipload to run ashore for customers like Parson Woodforde.

Pixley, who had the bizarre nickname of 'Cursemother', had further adventures which made him something of folk-hero. While at Flushing he heard news that an English ship carrying coal to the Continent had been intercepted off the coast of Holland by a French privateer which put a prize crew aboard. Pixley was British, albeit an outlaw, and he was having none of that. He gathered a crew, manned a cutter and put out to sea in quest of the Frenchman and his prize. He found him, fought him and came back triumphantly with the English brigantine, '. . . and has her now in his Custody in Flushing Harbour.'

As to the kind of craft available on the Norfolk coast, the smuggler had the services of some of the best boat-builders in a nation renowned for its excellence in the art. In *Once Upon a Tide* Hervey Benham describes the kind of craft they could turn out: 'the crowning glory of the Suffolk and Norfolk coast was the great clinker-built lugger, running up to sixty feet for fishing purposes and as much as eighty feet among the salvaging yawls, three-masted up to about 1840 and two-masted thereafter. Despite their considerable size and the fact that the fishermen were of course fully decked, they always retained the impression of being big *boats*, lithe and lovely hulls with the simplest as well as the most powerful of sailing gear.' From such a description it is quite easy to see why such 143 a lugger, loaded with contraband, could show a Revenue cutter a clean pair of heels.

In facing the perils of the deep there was an unwritten law which united 'runners' and Revenue. Late in November 1838 the Revenue cutter *Badger*, commanded by Lieut. R. Perceval of the Royal Navy, tailed the Dutch sloop *Volharden*, which was weighed well down in the water. The Revenue men boarded it in heavy weather and found a large cargo of contraband spirits. They transferred the smugglers to the cutter and put a prize crew aboard the sloop.

In getting back to port *Badger* was caught by the weather and, short of crew, was floundering on the edge of a real crisis when the prisoners came forward to offer their assistance. Their seamanship brought *Badger* back from the brink of disaster. When the case came to court in Yarmouth and two of the crew of smugglers were sentenced to six months' imprisonment, the cutter's captain spoke up for them. He told of their willing co-operation in the battle against the storm and asked the magistrates to show mercy. As a result their sentences were halved.

If we are to believe Athol Forbes in his *The Romance of Smuggling* (1909) a similar instance of unity in adversity occurred at the beginning of the 19th century. The captain of a naval warship had a disastrous encounter with a Frenchman three times it size. Damaged, and with many men dead and wounded, the ship put in to a Norfolk bay where the captain came ashore to seek help from civilians – and consolation from his fiancée, daughter of the Vicar of Gorleston. Leaving her father and the captain to talk, the girl made a four-mile dash to Corton Gap where she knew the local men had gathered to help in a big landing of contraband. Their response was immediate, they hastened to the scene, helped make the ship seaworthy, rigged jury-sails and supplemented the crew; they then sailed the ship out to meet the Frenchman once again and finally sent it to the bottom after an epic shoot-out.

Athol Forbes was in fact the pseudonym of the Reverend Forbes Phillips who was, in a later age, Vicar of Gorleston. He wrote very candidly of the vicarage and that former incumbent:

144   'I live on a part of the coast that is nearest to Holland, and

The wreck of a merchantman blown ashore on the Norfolk coast by the Victorian artist J. J. Hissey.

therefore conveniently situated for running the "stuff", and I live in a house that was constructed with a view not only of the Yarmouth Roads and the North Sea, but a further one of plundering the Revenue, and with the definite object of conveniences for this particular work. Beneath my feet as I write are large and roomy cellars, once used for the storage of imported goods, and until a few years ago a subterranean passage connected these with a landing-stage by the waterside: and let full truth be told, the designer of all was the vicar of the parish, and this house was, and is still, the vicarage.'

In one of his stories, told rather as fiction than as fact, he tells of the landing of a cargo in dead of night, describing how each person has his appointed task:

'A tall, elderly man, with a manner that would do credit to an alderman, ticks off things in a note-book, assisted by several men who rush hither and thither. He asks his questions quietly, and sees that he gets satisfactory replies; occasionally he intervenes to redirect some of the men in their running to and fro. Standing near, with his back to the wind and keeping the light on the book, is a man with a lantern. He rebukes a man for swearing, and it is not resented.

145

'Presently there is an interruption. A man appears in the midst of the busy scene demanding in loud tones what it all means. He is a new-comer to the neighbourhood and holds peculiar moral views.

'"Smuggling!" he shouts. "Smuggling! Oh, the shame of it! Is there no magistrate at hand. No justice of the peace?"'

'A sailor man trundling a cask of sugar knocks him aside, but still the questions are shouted with vigour. The wind blows the sand down his throat, but he proclaims his mission still: "Is there no clergyman, no minister, no . . .?"'

'"There's the vicar," says a fisherman, who thinks it's a case of sudden sickness.

'"Where? How far off does he live?" The questioner is prepared to go in search of him.

'"That's him, a-holding the lanthorn," was the reply.'

Towards the end of the period the method of sinking contraband in tubs and waterproof wrappings found favour on this coast, following its introduction in the Essex creeks and estuaries, but there were still some bloody confrontations between smugglers and Revenue men. In April 1816 a real battle took place at Caister in the course of an attempted landing. Mr Toby, the local Supervisor of the Excise, was so violently attacked that he lost the sight of an eye. This was typical of the encounters which moved Charles Harper, in *Smugglers* of 1909, to write 'which shows – if we had occasion to show – that the East Anglian could on occasion be as ferocious as the rustics of the South.'

8
From Stiffkey to King's Lynn

Stiffkey's claim to fame is the 'Stewkey Blue', a cockle, dredged by the thousand from the shallows off the saltmarshes which have accumulated behind the sheltering arm of Blakeney Point. In the village itself the old Elizabethan hall was largely burnt out in the 18th century. At that time the village, with its main street running parallel to the Stiffkey Brook, was remote and practically self-sufficient; people passing through from Cley to the east and Wells to the west would have been considered foreigners.

While Stiffkey had its cockles and those shining sands where farmers sent their men with carts to gather land-enriching seaweed, Wells-Next-The-Sea was able to boast a proper port at the head of a creek, with a quay where the Revenue cutter tied up, and merchantmen came in from journeys across the North Sea from ports in countries stretching from Scandinavia down to France.

The old harbour at Wells is a pool now, known as Abraham's Bosom. The saltmarshes stretch northward to form the east bank of the creek; in conjunction with the tide, they provided a labyrinth of escape routes for small-boat smugglers when the Revenue cutter was in the offing. West of Wells past Holkham Bay the marshy foreshore persists, but there are creeks – as at Overy Staithe where the former busy harbour is now much silted up. A few miles due south inland is Burnham Thorpe, the birthplace, in 1758, of Horatio Nelson.

Strung out around Brancaster Bay are Brancaster itself, Titchwell, Thornham and Holmes-Next-The-Sea, looking out across saltmarshes and such broad, broad beaches that they can hardly be called seaside beaches. Thornham's harbour,

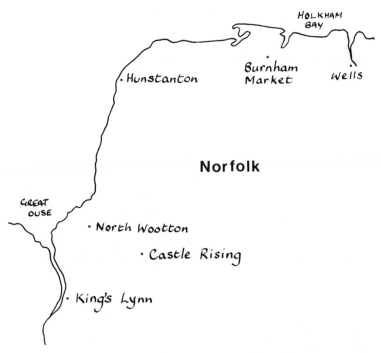

Places associated with smuggling in North West Norfolk.

which would have seen many a furtive figure slipping ashore across a crowd of boats, clutching his contraband, is now so silted up that it is used only rarely by the odd sailor more curious than commercial.

Where the coast turns sharply on the corner of the Wash stands Hunstanton, facing west. The modern seaside resort is Hunstanton St Edmund. The place the smugglers knew is Old Hunstanton, with its narrow streets and its ancient church of St Mary on the cliffs looking down from some 60 feet to a wide and sandy beach. The currents which wash those cliffs and clean the sand lose their impetus where the shoreline runs south, and the Wash is fringed by marshes which have been formed by the slow-moving Great Ouse draining off the Fens. Here King's Lynn grew into an important port and centre of

148

commerce; as the nearest seaport to Birmingham, it served the needs of a vast area of the Midlands.

King's Lynn has retained its port and its docks even though the sea has receded and the channel of the Great Ouse has to be dredged to keep the approaches open. As a port and a market town it serves a wide area through a web of roads radiating east, south and west, and linked with the long, straight track of the Peddar's Way between Ringstead and Castle Acre, which was ideally suited to the smugglers' system of stealthy transport, after dark, of things which no Lynn man talked about.

The beautiful Custom House built in 1683 by Henry Bell, the same master architect who designed the Duke's Head which still graces the Tuesday Market Place, is a reminder of those days when there seemed to be a duty of one sort or another to be paid on every commodity a ship brought in, and the King's Officers were there to see that importers paid those dues. In that same Custom House one can read records of those days, prized and preserved by the present 'Collector' of Her Majesty's Customs, who has them on loan from the Archivist of the central repository at the London Custom House.

These records are far from complete. What exists today are those few volumes which have escaped the fire, flood, war and wear of time and circumstance. Once such volume is the Letter Book of the little Custom House at Wells – an outlier, for Customs purposes, of the Collector of the Port of King's Lynn. It records all the communications received from the Board of Commissioners via the London Custom House. Unfortunately the volume which would have recorded the local Collector's queries and replies no longer exists. This letter-book covers the years 1660 to 1705 and is written in strong, black handwriting which is now difficult to interpret. An example of the business it dealt with is contained in the entry for 29 July 1663 when the Commisioners declared:

'I doe hereby order for the better management of his Maties. Service yt none of the Kings waytors or other officers in the Port of London or any other the Ports of England, Wales [etc.] ... shall at any time hereafter ... permitt ... any wines Tobacco Silkes wrought or any other goods or merchandise   149

King's Lynn Custom House, built in 1683. As a port and market town with a good network of roads leading to the Midlands and London, it made an ideal centre for smuggling.

whatsoever to bee landed but in the presence of one of the Officers commissioned by the Grand Farmer of his Maties. Customes & yt the said Grand Farmers & Officers have copies of such ... warrant [and that they] ... doe not take any Port Bonds or security for the Coasts or passe any Certificates but by & with the approbacion & consent of the Collectors for the Grand Farmers & yt none of his Maties. serchers doe shipp any of the said goods & merchandise for exportation but in the presence of one of the officers commissioned by the said grand farmers ... I doe hereby charge ... all his Maties. officers whome it may concern ... to observe & performe the same ... as they will answer the contrary at their Perills & as they value their places & to the end yt all his Maties. said officers may have the knowledge hereof his Maties. said Farmers ... are directed to send Copies hereof to all the said outports to bee there published & set upp in the severall Custom houses there.'

The Collector at Wells had a great deal more than smuggling to deal with. In 1665 he had an order that both sulphur

150

and saltpetre had to be added to the long list of items which had to be particularly looked out for: these two items were the constituents of gunpowder and their export at this time could give advantage to the Dutch with whom Britain was then at war.

Another entry in August 1677 supports the claim that smugglers were active here from early times. Mr Godfrey, the Wells Collector, received another exhortation from the Commissioners: 'We are informed . . . yt a vessell arrived in yor. Port the 13th ditto halfe laden with Pann tyles, Bottles & some Payles & Chaires. On which no officer was putt on board . . . wee are jealous at this time of the yere (especially beinge towards Sturbridge faire time) yt some fine goods have been landed out of her, she beeing but halfe laden or yt underneath those goods, some fine goods bee concealed; wee therefore desire you to informe us who boarded her & how he satisfied himselfe yt there were no fine goods concealed under the other we allso desire your especiall care in such cases to prevent the Landing [of] fine goods without payment of Custome.'

In these early days there was already a two-fold reason for duty being charged on so many imported goods. In the first place the Government needed to raise an enormous amount of extra revenue to conduct the war against France. It seemed very reasonable, therefore, to tax the very items which in one way or another had their origin in that country, for such trade made profit and thus revenue for the French government. So the Collector at Wells, as at every other port, had to keep a register book of the taxes they collected on 'all French wines, vinegar, brandy, linnen cloth, silks, salt, paper, and all manufactures made of or mixt with silke, thred, wooll, gold or silver or leather being of the growth or product or manufacture of any of the Dominions . . . of the French Kinge . . . during the term of three years'.

All through the years covered by these records the theme of smuggling and its prevention recurs again and again, and the Customs officers are regularly harangued on the subject, as in the autumn of 1679: 'considering now this season of the yeare [attempts would be made to] clandestinely bring in & putt on shore French wines & other French prohibited goods (as allso other wines & goods) yt ought to pay customs to the great 151 decimation of his Maties. revenues wee direct you ... use utmost diligence for prevention thereof'. To encourage the seizure of such contraband the officer who spotted the goods and confiscated them would, in the case of wine, get an allowance of five per cent of the value. A suitable allowance for the seizure of other prohibited goods was at that time being urgently considered. What is more, it was further laid down that a Customs officer could demand the help of the local constable in searching, in daytime, 'all shopp warehouses, cellers & other places' for such goods.

Despite these encouragements the Board of Commissioners had to address Mr Godfrey quite severely on 16 November 1680: 'We have received information of great quantities of Lynnen are presently landed & stolen on shoare in creekes & other places within the district of your Porte, wee therefore give you this admonition yt you & Mr. Rampley use all diligence & watchfullnesse to prevent those fraudulent practices.'

There were also occasions, not so often acknowledged by the Board, when the Wells Custom House officers did make searches which resulted in the seizure of contraband. The report by Mr Godfrey of one such incident brought the reply: 'Wee commend you & the Landwaiters diligence in discovering the 10 peeces of Lynnen with severall small casks fitted to be run which were privately concealed in the ketch arrived in your Port from Rotterdam, which you have secured in the Kings warehouse. If the Merchant shall desire to enter the said Lynnen & wines you may admitt entry thereof uppon paymt. of his Maties. duties, if they bee not French.'

A good example of the way in which the sailors of accredited merchant vessels indulged in a little opportunist smuggling is shown in the report by Mr Godfrey that his men had discovered 28 casks of wine and brandy 'on board Woodrowes vessell from Rotterdam which were unreported by the Master & found concealed under his Pann tyles after he had delivered part of his ladeing'. The advice from the Board on how to deal with this contraband and the ship shows, incidentally, some of the complications of the many regulations in force under the various Acts, all of which had to be remembered and enforced by the Collector and his men:

152

'The 12 small casks of Brandy are to bee executed upon the late Act, being imported in casks under 60 gallons, And the Sherry and Malaga wine uppon the clause on the Act for preventing of frauds, being imported from Holland, as allso the thirteen small casks of wine if they were other than Rhenish; the vessel is likewise forfeited by the said Act & we direct you to lay your hands uppon her in order to her prosecution.'

It has to be remembered that some of the Custom House men at the sharp end of confrontation with the smugglers were humble enough people, without the advantage of more than a very limited education. A very deliberately written note appears in the letter book among all those important exhortations from above:

'I Jno. Bloome doe sweare to be true & faithful in ye charge & execution of ye Office committed to my charge as Boatman & Tidesman in their Matie's service at Wells. So help me God. John Bloome.'

It was not Bloome who wrote this but one of his superiors. The boatman could only just manage to write his own signature and we can imagine the slow business he made of that, with his tongue between his teeth as he pushed the unfamiliar quill across the paper.

At this period the smuggling gangs were getting organised. In January 1692 a general order was issued from the London Custom House that they had heard that 'Great quantities of French wines have been bought upp in France in order to be imported into the Kingdom from St. Sebastian, Bilboa & other places' – warning all Customs officers to be on their guard. Not that the Custom House at Wells had much of a staff to guard the coast; in 1693 the staff had to sign affidavits concerning their future employment, and from these we can see that Owen Godfrey as Collector was supported by a Comptroller or Deputy, Roger Pedley; John Bloome was the Boatman at Wells and John Wood filled the same post at Blakeney and Cley. The third Boatman was Robert Thetford.

The following year it was necessary to advise all Customs officers to be on the look-out for the latest ploy introduced by the smugglers – using molasses barrels to smuggle in brandy. The Commissioners even took the seasonal nature of the 153 wine trade into consideration. In November 1700 they issued a warning: 'This beeing ye Season of ye yeare wherein new wynes will be Imported from abroad' Collectors were to take great care that all French wines be refused entry. They were not to be deceived by the fact that such wines might be artificially coloured, and imported through other countries such as Portugal and Italy to disguise their true origin.

These Letter Books, official and impersonal as they are, cannot reflect the real, raw life of the smuggler and Revenue man in the port and off the coast of Wells-Next-The-Sea. Imagine the rumours that flew around the small town concerning one episode in the long story.

When the well-known Revenue cutter *Walpole* went out on a patrol from Wells in June 1731 with Joseph Southgate, the mate, temporarily in command, it was involved in a very nasty incident. Southgate guessed that two French 'shallops' he came up with were the ships which had been distributing contraband brandy among a fleet of colliers from Newcastle, then waiting for a favourable wind off Burnham. The shallops quickly proved his suspicions were correct; one opened fire on the *Walpole* while the other tried to ram it with a view to boarding it and engaging in a hand-to-hand battle. Southgate managed to draw away from them both and got his ship into Holkham Bay, but then the Frenchmen overhauled him, boarded the *Walpole* and overwhelmed the crew. They dragged Southgate on to one of their boats and brought him face-to-face with the Englishman, Peters, a hardened and violent smuggler. He had mistaken Southgate for Captain Harrold, who was normally the commander of the Yarmouth sloop and had given Peters a hard time. The smuggler had declared a vendetta against him and was about to plunge his sword into Southgate when he realised Southgate was not the man he wanted. He let him go, telling him to pass on the death threat to his captain. In fact Captain Harrold died a natural death shortly afterwards, so Peters' violent threats could not be carried out.

Some 50 years after Southgate so narrowly escaped death a man was buried with full military honours in the churchyard at Hunstanton. He was so honoured because he was a soldier killed in action, and the stone erected over his grave tells all:

In Memory of William Webb, late of the 15th Lt. D'ns.,
who was shot from his horse by a party of Smugglers
on the 26th of Sepr. 1784.
I am not dead, but sleepeth here,
And when the Trumpet Sound I will appear.
Four balls thro' me Pearced there way:
Hard it was. I'd no time to pray
This stone that here you do see
My Comerades erected for the sake of me.

An Excise officer was also killed in this desperate affair, and in due course two smugglers, William Kemble and Andrew Gunton, were brought to justice. They were clearly the murderers, but much to everybody's surprise the jury pronounced them not guilty. Such was the strength of feeling in the neighbourhood for the smugglers and the service they offered in the way of luxury goods at much-reduced prices. The prosecution did not let the case rest; they asked for a new trial, their counsel angrily declaring that 'If a Norfolk jury were determined not to convict persons guilty of the most obvious crimes, simply because, as smugglers, they commanded the sympathy of the country people, there was an end to all justice.' The court agreed to the application, a new jury was appointed and all the evidence was repeated. The jury took three hours to bring out their verdict – and once again it was 'not guilty'. So the murderous smugglers went free.

Back in the Custom House at Lynn the modern visitor will see that where the old Wells letter books finish, those of King's Lynn take over, running from 1712 to 1724. The Custom House at Lynn dealt with a multitude of administrative and executive matters involved in the day-to-day collection of dues on a long list of dutiable goods. It also had to find men and ships and time to fight what could be considered a guerilla war waged by the highly-organised smugglers.

In the year that these records begin there are reports of hampers of wine seized from otherwise honest merchant ships' captains with properly declared cargoes. A notice from the Board tells the Revenue men to look out for 'Linnen, spice and other goods concealed in reels of cable yarn'. A report for the quarter ending at Christmas sets out the strength of the Lynn 155 customs service – and it seems a thin line to hold back the smugglers and deal with everyday affairs at the same time. The salaries shown are altogether too remote from the modern value of the pound for us to appreciate their significance:

Collector	Henry Hare		
Surveyor	Tho. Turner		£12.10s.
Riding Surveyor from Wells to Linn	Fra. Chaloner		15.00s.
Waiters & Searchers	Geo. Butler		
	Alexr. Gamble	3 each £8.15s	
	Alexr. Middleton		26.5s.
Tidesmen	Phil. Butler		
	Fras. Bateman	5 each £3.15s	
	Richd. Cooke		
	John Lacheur		18.15s.
Boatmen	Wm. Clay		
	Jno. Purdy	4 each £6.5s.	
	Robt. Everard		
	Tho. May		25.00s.
			£102.10s.

Just a month later the need for such a staff was amply demonstrated. Thomas Crompton, master of *Peace* of King's Lynn, was heading for his home port after a voyage to Rotterdam when called on to stop by the Customs yacht. He obviously lost his temper, and allowed his vessel to foul the Customs boat to the extent that it was ultimately rendered unserviceable. The Revenue men therefore made a very thorough search and confiscated a small amount of brandy, ten 'East India handkerchiefs' and two small canisters of tea. This was hardly an economic success; the yacht had been put out of commission, so further searches at sea could not be made, with inevitable loss of revenue. The Board had their agents looking for a suitable replacement for the next two months, and though they looked as far afield as Plymouth they had, in the end, to agree to a boat being specially built.

Over that period the Riding Officer would have been all the more important in checking that smuggling did not go on wholesale in the absence of any deterrent at sea. Just what this man was expected to do is set out in a document sent out from the London Custom House in July 1717:

'Instructions to Jeffery Mann, Riding Surveyor from Wells to Linn Regis, to reside at Hunston [Hunstanton].

'1. You are once in every week at least and oftner as occasion shall require to visit the Coast and places within your District, and as often as you come to Wells or Linn, You are to notify to the Collector of those ports your being there, and take care that a Memorial thereof be entred in their Journal Books.

'2. To the end that We may have a clear Account how you do Imploy time, and what Services have been done by you, you are at the end of every Calendar Month to make up a journal expressing where you were every day, and what Services have been performed by you, and to deliver such a journal signed by you within three days after ye end of every month to the Collr. of Linn to be by him transmitted to us.

'3. You are to consult with the Collector & Officers of Wells & Linn on all occasions for ye better carrying on Her Majesties Service.

'4. You are to take particular care to prevent the Running of Spices, Linnens & other Goods which we are informed are frequently smugled within your District especially against Sturbridge Fair and therefore you are to apply yourself diligently to ye discovery of those Frauds and to make Seizure of all such prohibited Goods which you find imported contrary to Law, and all such Customable Goods as you shall find Landed without Payment of Custom whereof you are to inform us.'

Even the Collector himself, Henry Hare, was given a set of rules for the conduct of his business as Collector. Rule number 2 of a list sent out in 1715 gives an insight into the system of incentive bonus then in operation: 'Whenever you or any other Officer within ye Port shall Ride or perform any Service whatsoever upon Informacion given of Goods Run, or intended to be Run, or in Looking out in Hopes of making Seizures, you are not either for yourself or such Offrs. to earn an Allowance for ye same, the Law having given you to Seize a Share of ye Penalties & Forfeitures as an Encouragement & Recompence for yt. Service.'

After a further admonition to greater vigilance, 'It having

been represented to the Commissioners that great quantities of Bengal raw silks are frequently run on your coast out of vessels from Holland', Mr Hare was able to report the seizure of 93 gallons of brandy, 12 gallons of wine, eight of rum and 11 pounds of chocolate. Even then the Board felt that a further warning was necessary, to the effect that smugglers were at that time in Holland buying up goods brought in by the big merchant ships from the Dutch East Indies, and that it was expected that large landings would be attempted on the Norfolk coast.

That there was still money to be made in the smuggled export of English wool is apparent from the Commissioners' expression of concern about 'Ships Hovering on the Coast waiting for opportunity to run their Cargos of Brandy & other goods and to carry off Wooll.' This is further supported by the general circular to all Collectors to look out for 'Jas. Carron Master of a French Vessell [which] took in 45 packs of Wooll at Torrington Hole & carryed the same to Calais in France and . . . is daily expected on Your Coast with 25 hogsheads & 200 half anchors of Brandy and other goods with intention to run the same.'

In 1717 the Custom smack was re-commissioned by a special warrant on 17 July. It was around 40 tons burthen and carried a crew consisting of a commander (Robert Day), a mate, three 'Marriners' and a boy. Not, one would think, a very large force to contend with the much larger boats and crews of smugglers armed to the teeth and determined to resist arrest. The annual cost of the smack, in terms of the crew's pay and food, was reckoned at £137.17s.2¼d.

Even the Board admitted that 'the Officers are very often Affronted, Abused, Assaulted & Obstructed in the Execution of their Duty.' They encouraged their Collectors to prosecute those responsible whenever they possibly could and brought in a regulation which would give informers one third of the officer's share of the appraised value of seized goods. At this time the Wisbech Customs officers were having such a hard time of it, being 'very much Beaten & obstructed in ye Execution of their Duties by Joseph Spencer, Master of the Wisbich from Rotterdam, a Master of a Barge and others', that the King's Lynn Collector was instructed to 'repair to Wisbich and Assist the Officers in ye Discovering and Apprehending the severall offenders'.

During this same year of 1718 Henry Hare was able to report that the Revenue smack confiscated nine half-ankers of Brandy out of the *Mary* of Lynn; two half-ankers from the *Desire* of Lynn and, by the vigilance of Jasper Bayly and William Taylor, five half-ankers that were found already unloaded on the beach. All of them had been safely stowed in the Custom warehouse prior to their sale, which would enrich the national exchequer and also reward the officers concerned.

On 6 October a much more serious incident occurred. Mr Hare reported it to London and received the reply from the Board that, having his report of 'some of the Officers having made seizures of 11 half Ankers of Brandy from a house, the same has been rescued from them in a very riotous manner and they much beaten and abused in the execution of their duty by severall people of the Town, some of them are committed to gaol by the Magistrates for ye said offence and wee direct that you take the most proper opportunity to thank the sd. Magistrates in the name of the Board'. It is quite obvious that conviction and punishment of smugglers went so much against the feelings of local people, even those as well off as the magistrates themselves, that such direct action was unusual and was to be encouraged in every way. The Board must have felt their expression of appreciation to the magistrates was worthwhile when they heard that the smugglers were convicted and ordered to be whipped round the town. The Collector and his men must have watched the scene with some satisfaction from the very Custom House wherein that Letter Book is kept today.

The mate of the Revenue smack, Joseph Skeats, reported in 1719 that he had taken in charge a boat in which he had found 'a considerable quantity of tea and spices in stone bottles'. This was an unusual disguise for these items and represented a serious attempt to deceive the Customs. He was ordered to take the usual action in court to have, not only the contraband, but also the boat itself confiscated and sold or destroyed according to the Collector's discretion. Another capture in

159

that year included quantities of brandy, rum, mace, coffee, tea, nutmegs and wine, as well as the yawl and the lighter in which they were found.

Up on this coast there were numerous French and Dutch smugglers awaiting their chance to put contraband ashore, to the extent that the Customs officers were told that they could call on the commanders of Royal Navy ships in the area to assist in dealing with any threat by armed men determined to land goods within the limits of their ports. The Dutch had devised a crafty way of getting their goods ashore, as comes out in a Commissioners' letter of 21 June 1722: 'The Commissioners being informed that it is a practice for the Holland sloops and such traders to put great part of their Goods which they design to Run on board some Fishing Boat or other Vessell when they come near the Coast & when the officers are pursuing and attending the Sloops to rummage them at a Distance the Small Vessells and Boats take the opportunity to Run the Goods ashoar.' The officers were instructed by the Commissioners to keep a 'Watchfull Eye'! Down to the last page of the letter book in July 1724 there is constant mention of undescribed goods seized which had then to be legally assigned to confiscation and subsequent sale or destruction, along with the smugglers' boats, with any moneys arising to be paid into the Exchequer.

From 1724 there is a virtual gap in the records for almost a hundred years. There are a few scattered references to this period in newspapers which are themselves hard to find, and in one or two documents preserved in the archives of the County Record Office. One such document has some significance in demonstrating how the smugglers' activities could cause trouble and worry to innocent folk over a wide area. In this instance it all started on a lovely last day of July in 1773 at North Wotton, now more commonly written Wootton, a village just north of King's Lynn.

Richard Fawsell had a farm there, 'part whereof lies contiguous to the Bank of the Great Navigable River or Channel leading to King's Lynn'. That morning Fawsell's shepherd came to him and said that some of the farmer's men had found 'some liquor in a crop of wheat', which was growing on land near the sea bank. Fawsell went to see his men and check on what they were doing. He was annoyed and disturbed to find three of them 'lying on the ground near the Gate of the said Land, and a small Cask lying by them which they had nearly emptied of the Liquor', which he learned was gin, 'And one of them being very much disguised therewith.' Fawsell asked them what they had found, 'Whereupon they fetched from a small distance three casks'. The farmer judged them to be half-ankers. He told his men to carry them up to his house at once. He neither tasted the contents of these casks nor allowed anyone else to do so.

Then, 'being totally ignorant of the Laws relating to the Revenue, he did resolve to take some good advice what he ought to do'. So the next morning he set aside all his farm work to go to Lynn and see an attorney. (His men would not have been capable of doing much work that day either.) The advice he received was to give information as soon as possible to an officer of the Excise. He could not accomplish this on the same day, so he returned home determined to go to the Custom House on the day following. It was evening when he got home to tell his wife all about it, but she had even more important news for him: a man had called at the house in his absence, had asked for the casks and left word that he would be waiting at the local alehouse for the farmer to go and see him.

Fawsell went there with the greatest apprehension, fully justified, for this man, a smuggler, said 'That the persons who claimed the property of the said Liquor at the said Alehouse in the Hearing of the Landlord & his Wife threatened Vengeance against any persons who should be the means of depriving them of it And declared they would Fire every House in the Town if they had not the Liquor again.' He so intimidated the farmer that he did not dare go to the Custom House and report either the find or the subsequent meeting with one of the smugglers. He was convinced that they would have set fire to his house or barns – such acts had been carried out with impunity in other places.

He went home in despair, and his frame of mind was not improved when he was told that his men had found more casks in the wheat and in the field of beans adjoining it. He did absolutely nothing about it, and told the men to leave the

161

casks just where they were. That same evening a man called at his house again and asked for the three casks he had in his possession. Fawsell did not dare to refuse. He produced them and this man and others carried them away. Since the casks in the corn also disappeared he presumed that the smugglers had retrieved them as well.

News like this flew round the village and on down to King's Lynn. It reached the ears of the officers in the Custom House, and the farmer was accused of being party to the smuggling and guilty of the concealment and subsequent disposal of the casks at his house. This was the reason for the document, which is headed: 'To the Honourable Commissioners of his Majesty's Revenue of Excise the Humble Petition of William Fawsell of North Wotton in the County of Norfolk, Farmer.' The last paragraph of the document makes a very sensible point:

'That a Capias directed to the Sheriff of Norfolk has been issued against your Petitioner for a Forfeiture of Ninety six pounds thereby alledged to be Incurred by your Petitioner whereupon your Petitioner being lately arrested, was obliged to give Bail for his Appearance at the Return of the said Writt, which Bail was given by your Petitioner for no other Reason but to prevent his being carried to prison, and to obtain time for making his Application to your Honours by Petition – And your Petitioner being informed that the utmost Penalty he could incur by Law is the treble Value of the Goods, cannot guess why he is charged with a Penalty of Ninety six pounds as the said Casks were only what are commonly called half Anchors, containing about five gallons each, the full Value whereof as he believes is not above Six or Seven Shillings per Gallon.'

The poor man humbly prayed that the Excise would drop its case against him. He even offered to pay the reasonable cost of the contents of those three casks as a penalty for his ignorance of the laws and his failure to report the incident at once. So we see the ripples of trouble spreading from the spot where the smugglers chose to land their contraband. One would hope that the petitioner was leniently dealt with by the law, but unfortunately the outcome is not recorded.

This anecdote can be nicely balanced by another concern-

ing a place at the other end of Norfolk – Earsham, on the bank
of the Waveney and the border of the county just west of
Bungay. In 1771, just one year before the event just described,
a man named Mark Butcher had a large vault erected in the
churchyard. The Reverend G. Sandby, a principal officer of
the ecclesiastical court of the Diocese of Norwich, was asked to
make enquiries. He reported back:

'I have both made Inquiry into the Affair I Mention'd to
you, and view'd the Mausoleum, myself.

'At Easter last Mark Butcher was chosen to be one of the
Churchwardens of Earsham, and the only one sworn into
Office. This, he thought, gave him Power to do what he wou'd
within the Fences of the Church-yard. Accordingly, he
directed his Landlord Lane, Stone-Mason at Norwich, to hew
him out a stately Monument for the Family of the Butchers,
whereof the Chief is said to be a great Smugler. Some say the
Vault will contain 8, some say ten, and some fifteen coffins;
and some suspect that it will contain very different things. The
Vault is about 10f½ in Length by 8f; and what is above
Ground, and done by Lane, is all of Stone. The Bricks us'd
within were, as I am informed 2600, which were laid by John
Doughton of Bungay, and his Labourer John Reeve ... It
seems to me improper to pass by this Offence; but I wait for
such advice as you shall be pleas'd to give.'

The advice sought was given in September 1772; that since
Butcher had the monument erected without obtaining a
licence from the church authorities he must tear it down again
and fill up the hole which had been excavated. What we shall
never know now is whether it was originally intended to serve
as a very innocent-looking warehouse for contraband, or
whether the smuggling family had grown so rich from the
proceeds of their illicit trade that they could afford to be
buried in the style of landed gentry.

The amount of smuggling that went on, and the distance
inland to which the contraband travelled is quite surprising,
bearing in mind the primitive transport available, and the
need for secrecy, or at least discretion. It has been seen how
brandy and gin turned up regularly at Parson Woodforde's
Rectory at Weston Longville. The Lopham villages are as far
away again as that from any point on the coast, lying as they

163

Earsham Churchyard, where one Mark Butcher had a suspiciously large vault erected, large enough to store quantities of illicit goods in transit.

do between Thetford and Diss, yet even here the attraction of cheaper liquor made business for the smuggler.

In 1786 Thomas Cock, keeper of an alehouse at Lopham, unwittingly wrote his name in the history of Norfolk by the simple process of assaulting and obstructing three Excise officers. The official record runs: 'That on the Twentyseventh day of May last Thomas Cock the Younger of Lopham ... Alehouse keeper did assault and obstruct the said James Lea, Henry Coates and Samuel Christmas being then in the due Execution of their Offices.' It goes on to say that anybody who knew Cock's whereabouts was to see that he appeared before a judge or a justice of the peace to be bound in the sum of £100 paid by him and £50 paid by two other sureties to answer in the Court of the King's Bench the charge mentioned above. Cock was found and taken before a J.P. but he refused to put up the bail, so he was lodged in the prison in Norwich Castle. It can only be presumed that Cock had something to hide when the Excise men called – and it is reasonable to assume that, as an alehouse keeper, Cock would be very interested in the acquisition of cheap brandy and gin.

Through the final years of the 18th century and into the 19th the smuggling continued on this part of the coast, though apparently to a lesser degree. By 1834, when the 'Board and Officers Letterbook of the King's Lynn Custom House' takes up the story for the next seven years, the Collector was reporting, on 17 January: 'Hon. Sirs, In obedience to the Direction contained in the secretary's Letter of the 15th Inst. No. 8. requiring us to report forthwith and especially on the subject of Smuggling. We beg leave to state that the Practice of Smuggling is by no means increased on the District, for we have no intelligence of, nor any suspision that any run of contraband Goods had been effected or attempted thereon for some time past.

'And with reference to your Honours confidential communication of the 9th Inst. stating that Information has been received that a disguised vessel or Smack from this Port or Boston would attempt at a Landing on the Yorkshire coast. We cannot learn that any such vessel is missing from the port, but we understand that the ADELAIDE late tender to the REDBREAST Cutter has been sold at Boston and is now in the hands of a Smuggling connection there, and as she is a vessel adapted for such a purpose it is probable she may be so employed.'

This was followed in the March report by a reiteration that 'we have no information or suspicion that any run of Contraband Goods has been effected or attempted in the District in the last qtr. and to this effect is the Report which we herewith transmit of the Coast Officer at the Out-Station of Heacham. We have understood, however, that though ourselves actually free from them, attempts of this nature have been made on the neighbouring Districts both to the Eastward & Westward of us, and on the latter [the Lincolnshire Coast] the Smugglers have been checked in their illegal traffic by prosecutions which have weakened, if not entirely crippled the party.'

These records also provide proof of the method of licensing boats to keep control of smuggling, as well as the continuing check on the dimensions of boats. On 30 April 1834 the Collector wrote:

'Enclosed we transmit Certs. of the Dimensions of the Boats undermentioned belonging to this Port. The owners of which request your Honours Licence for their employment, We beg leave to state that each of the Owners of these boats was engaged in a Smuggling transaction some years since, and these Licences have in consequence thereof been limited to <u>one</u> year, but we have not heard of their having subsequently been concerned or suspected of smuggling –

Thomas & Lucy   Wm. Sentor, Owner
Mary   Wm. Sentor, Owner.'

Although the running and landing of contraband as a cargo in itself had practically ceased owing to the reorganisation of the Coastguard and its increased watchfulness, there were still many masters of trading vessels who were not above smuggling goods in under the cover of lawful trading. In 1839 the Board of Commissioners received an anonymous letter from a person signing himself 'Fair Play', which paints a vivid picture of corruption:

166

'June 26th 1839. Lynn Regis.

My Lords and Gentlemen.

Excuse the liberty I have taken with addressing you on the great quantity of Contraband Spirits, which is brought to this Port by vessels laden with timber from the Baltic. I should say the Revenue has been defrauded of not less than £2,000 a year from this Port for years past. Respecting a vessel named The Fate, the Master is known to be one of the greatest Vendors of Liquor and Tobacco and Cigars and has carried on in the most unblushing manner for years, and I do not hesitate to say that the greater part of the contraband spirits belonged to him and his son mate of the vessel also, and must know what was going on.

The collector of customs is near related to most of the owners of the Baltic traders from this Port and of course will write to you Gentlemen as favourably as possible, so that the ship should not be forfeited to the owner. And I know the officers who are put on board these vessels are related also to many of the Crews in this Trade And they are bribed with Liqueour and Tobacco. I have this information from one of the Officers who is distantly related to me and who says it is equal to one fourth of his salary. The whole Custom House Establishment ought to be removed from this Port immediately for giving the greatest encouragement to smuggling.

Signed   Fair Play.'

This bombshell aroused a considerable correspondence. The Collector had to send a holding reply and then make enquiries. In the first instance he refuted the accusation, saying that it must have been made by someone 'smarting under the measures we have adopted to detect the smuggling attempted lately and foiled'. Then he followed up with surveillance of the *Fate*, a search and a discovery of contraband. So the anonymous informer was right in that particular. The Master of the *Fate* was summoned to appear on a charge of smuggling on 29 July 1839. He was found guilty and fined £100 for having on board 'Brandy, Rum, Geneva, Sweet Spirits and Tobacco in Casks and Packages of illegal dimensions'. He had maintained that he knew nothing at all of the

Sails can still be seen alongside the quay at Wells-Next-The-Sea where two centuries ago the Collector in his Custom House carefully penned his reports.

contraband which must have been put on board by members of his crew. This plea was accepted and taken into account, and since he was carrying a perfectly legal cargo in the normal way of trade his boat was not confiscated. But he was reprimanded for his negligence and lack of vigilance over his crew and their use of his vessel for their own clandestine purposes. The court expressed the view that he retained his good name as an honest ship's master.

The close of the smuggling story in the area covered by the Collector of King's Lynn Custom House is best expressed in the words of the officer at Heacham reporting to that Collector on 11 October 1841:

'In submitting my Report as to the State of Smuggling on my District during the last qtr. I beg to state that from all the information upon the subject I can obtain, I am of the opinion that nothing of the kind has been attempted during the above period.'

Bibliography

Benham, Hervey *Last Stronghold of Sail* Harrap, 1948.

Benham, Hervey *Once Upon a Tide* Harrap, Rev. ed. 1971.

Benham, Hervey *The Smugglers' Century* Essex Record Office, 1986

Bensusan, S. L. *A Countryside Chronicle* 1907

Bishop, George *Observations, Remarks, and Means to Prevent Smuggling* 1783

Chelmsford Chronicle (later *Essex Chronicle*) from 1764

Cope, Sir John, Chairman. Report of the Parliamentary Committee of Enquiry, 1736

Day, James Wentworth *Coastal Adventure* Harrap, 1949

Defoe, Daniel *Tour Through the Whole Island of Great Britain* (3 vols) 1724–7

Dutt, W. A. *The Norfolk and Suffolk Coast* 1909

Forbes, Athol *The Romance of Smuggling* C. Arthur Pearson, 1909

Goodwin, William. Diaries 1785–1809 (MS)

Harper, Charles *Smugglers* (1909) Reprinted Frank Graham, 1966

Harriott, John *Struggles Through Life* (3 vols) 1808

Ipswich Journal from 1708

Leather, John *The Salty Shore* Dalton, 1979

Marryat, Capt. Frederick *The Three Cutters* 1836

Martin, Frank *Rogues' River* Ian Henry, 1983

Morley, Geoffrey *Smuggling in Hampshire & Dorset, 1700–1850* Countryside Books, 1983

Nicholls, F. F. *Honest Thieves* Heinemann, 1973

Roe, Fred *Essex Survivals* Methuen, 1929

Scott, J. M. *The Tea Story* Heinemann, 1964

Smith, Graham *King's Cutters: The Revenue Service & the War Against Smuggling* Conway Maritime Press, 1983

Smith, Graham *Something to Declare* Harrap, 1980

Thompson, Leonard P. *Smugglers of the Suffolk Coast* Bret Valley Publications, 1968. Reprinted Boydell, 1975

Walker, Kenneth *The History of Clacton* Clacton Urban District Council, 1966

Waugh, Mary *Smuggling in Kent & Sussex, 1700–1840* Countryside Books, 1985.

Weaver, Leonard *The Harwich Story* L. T. Weaver, 1975

Woodforde, Rev. James *The Diary of a Country Parson* Beresford, John (ed), (5 vols) O.U.P. 1926–1931

Wright, Thomas *A History of Essex* (2 vols) 1836

Transcripts of correspondence between the Board of Customs and its officers at Maldon, Colchester, Harwich, and Yarmouth can be seen in the Library of H. M. Customs and Excise. Those referring to Essex are duplicated in the Essex Record Office. Original records can be seen in the Public Record Office. Original records referring to the King's Lynn area, including Wells, are held on loan in the present Custom House at King's Lynn. Many of these records have been lost, some due to enemy action in the Second World War, so that the coverage of the whole period for Essex, Suffolk and Norfolk can only be described as intermittent.

Index

Aldeburgh 39, 97, 141
Aldis, John 69
Aldred, John 108
Aldringham 125
Ames, John 70
Anderson, James 50
Andrews, Richard 17, 137
Arnold, Coe 106
Ashby, Richard 93
Ashpole, Cornelius 96
Atterton, Billy 142

Bacon, Thomas 83
Bacton 131
Bailey, George 115
Baker, Robert 108
Ballard, Mr 128
Baring-Gould, Rev Sabine 62
Barking 32, 47
Barking Creek 47
Barr, James 69
Battle of Caister 146
Battlesbridge 62
Baxter, James 58
Bayfield, Mr 111
Bayly, Samuel 106
Beaumont Quay 68
Beccles 106
Benacre 103, 105, 109, 115, 118
Benacre Street 105
Benacre Warren 105
Benfleet 58
Benfleet Creek 47
Bentley, James 69

Best, George 40
Biggs, John 117
Billbo, Nicholas 55
Billericay 77
Birch Hall 68
Blakeney 131, 133, 140, 153
Blaxhall 124
Bloom, John 153
Blyth, William 52, 53
Boscawen, Captain 73
Boucher, Thomas 91
Bowles, Clumpy 123, 124
Bradley, Bill 64
Bradley, William Charles 63
Bradwell 48
Brancaster 147
Brandeston 121
Brandon 33
Brentwood 77
Brightlingsea 71, 79, 92
Brightlingsea Creek 65
Buck, John 16, 142
Buck, Robert 138
Buck, Thomas 81
Burdett, Mr 105
Burnham on Crouch 48, 55
Burnham Thorpe 147
Butcher, Mark 163

Caister 146
Cage, John 121, 122
Canvey Island 47
Cartwright, George 122
Castle Acre 149

Chapman, James 93
Chelmsford 63
Christmas, Samuel 165
Clacton 66, 67
Clement, Richard 97
Cley 131, 147, 153
Coates, Henry 165
Cock, Thomas 165
Cockett Wick 66
Colchester 63, 65, 71, 74, 77, 82
Colchester Custom House 76
Coldfair Green 124
Cole, William 77
Cooper, William 124, 125
Cope, Sir John 20, 26
Corbolt, Jack 104
Corringham 47
Corton Gap 144
Crabbe, George 39
Cribband, Thomas 91
Cromer 33, 128
Crompton, Thomas 156
Cross, John 112
Cullum, George 121
Cunningham, Rev Francis 141
Cursemother (alias John
    Pixley) 143

Dagnett, Captain Isaac 79, 95,
    97
Darby, Captain 103
Davies, Griffith 94
Davis, Mr 107
Deane, John 104
de Bardieux, Miss 89
Debney, 'Nosey' 124
Debney, Robert 124, 125
Decker, Isaac 69
Dedham Lock 38
Defoe, Daniel 45, 50
de Hynton, William 13
Dengie 48
de Okele, William 13
Deptford 46

Dodds, R 62
Dounygng, John 13
Dowsett, John 50
Dowsett, William 50, 51, 55
D'Oyley, Mr 92, 93
Dunn, Lieutenant 116
Dunn, Robert 107
Dunningworth 124
Dunwich 108, 109, 111, 141
Dyball, Samuel 106

Earl Soham 22
Earsham 163
Easey, J 125
East Mersea 62
East Tuddenham 142
Edgefield 140
Emberson, Mr 53, 55

Fambridge Ferry 56
Farrington, Philip 70
Fawsell, Richard 160, 161, 162
Fellowes, Crocky 123
Flag Creek 65
Flushing 56, 82, 143
Forbes, Athol 144
Foulness 59
Foxell, George 55
Francis, Mr 57
Francis, Christopher 55
Frans Green 142
Frinton 67
Friston 124
Fryer, Samuel 81

Garencies, Lieutenant 54
Geedon Creek 65
George Inn, Hadleigh 116
'Giffling' Jack Corbolt 104
Gildersleeves, R 125
Godfrey, Owen 151, 152
Golmer Gat 99
Gooding, John 69
Goodwin, William 22

Gorleston   103, 104, 144
Gravesend   45, 46, 59
Great Stambridge   48
Green Man, Tunstall   124
Gregory Gang   48
Grootham, Emanuel   69
Gunton, Andrew   154

Hadleigh Castle   50
Hadleigh Gang   116, 118, 120, 123
Hadleigh Marsh   47
Hadleigh Ray   47
Hamford Water   67
Happisburgh   128, 129, 131
Hardy, Rev Robert   142
Hare, Henry   157, 159
Harriott, John   53
Harris, Jeremiah   96
Harrold, Captain   107, 154
Hart, Captain Edward   52, 98, 99
Harvey, Captain   77, 99
Harvey, Daniel   79
Harvey, John   122, 123
Harwich   68, 87, 89, 91, 94
Hasborough   128
Havengore Church   48
Havergate Island   87
Hawley   121
Heacham   168
Hedge-End Island   68
Herring, Mr   105
Hewett, Samuel   32, 47
Hewett, Scrymgeour   47
Hewitt, Clerk   137
Hickling Broad   140
Hockley   57
Holkham Bay   147, 154
Holland Haven   67
Hollesley Bay   100
Holmes-Next-The-Sea   147
Honingham   138
Hopkins, Martin   100

Hornchurch   47
Horsey Island   68
Hullbridge   48
Hunstanton   33, 147, 154
Hunwick, Mr   37, 38
Hurrell, Helen   106
Hurrell, Henry   106

Ilford   40, 41, 77
Ingall, Mr   125
Ingate Stone   115
Inglish, John   115
Ipswich   87, 94, 115
Ipswich Custom House   87

Jackson Mr   104
Jacobs, Ben   115
Jarvis, Thomas   105
Jaywick   66
Johnson, Isaac   81

Kemble, William   154
Kesland Haven   105
Kessingland   118
Kettleborough   121
King, Adam   55
King's Beam House   14
King's Lynn   147, 148
King's Lynn Custom House   149, 154, 161–2, 165, 168
Kirby Creek   68
Kirby, John   79
Kirby-le-Soken   92
Knott, William   107

Landan, Anthony   97
Langham   135
Lanham, David   107
Landguard Point   85
Lavenham   33
Lea, James   165
Leather, John   54
Lee, Thomas   50
Lee Wick   66

Legate, Benjamin 137
Leigh 36, 47, 50, 58
Leigh Custom House 50
Leiston 118, 123, 124, 125
Lisle, William 70, 76
Little Oakley 68
Lopham 163, 165
Lord Orford 141
Loten, John 50
Lowndes, Mr 87

Major, John 96
Malden, Jeremy 91
Maldon 48, 50, 52, 59, 63
Mann, Jeffrey 157
Manningtree 68
Maplin Sands 48
Marryat, Captain 135
Marsh House 68
Martin, Captain Robert 69, 72, 73, 74, 78
Martlesham 43
Martlesham Creek 87
Massingham, John 112
Matthews, Mr 139
Mattishall Burgh 137
Mayes, William 70
Mortlock, James 91

Nelson, Horatio 147
Newson, Sam 123
Nichols, Thomas 69
Nicols, George 124
Northey Island 48
North Walsham 131
North Weir Point 87
North Wotton 160, 162
Norwich 131
Norwich Castle 105, 113, 165

Oates, Captain Christopher 109
Old Hall Marsh, Tollesbury 56
Old Swan Inn, Southwold 135
Orford 87

Orford Ness 32, 98, 100, 103
Orlibar, Mr 89
Osea Island 48
Overy Staithe 147
Oxley Marshes 87

Paglesham 48, 52, 55
Pakefield 109
Palgrave, William 127
Parkeston Quay 68
Parrot and Punchbowl, Aldringham 125
Parsons, Richard 95
Peddar's Way 149
Pedley, Roger 153
Peewit Island 68
Pennyhole Bay 67, 68
Perceval, Lieutenant R 144
Phillips, Captain 92, 93
Phillips, Rev Forbes 144
Pitt, William the Younger 27
Pixley, John 143
Pond Hall, Hadleigh 123
Preston, John 127
Prittlewell 47
Pulham, Mr 89
Pyefleet Channel 65

Rampley, Mr 152
Read, Mr 123
Ready, Rev 139, 140
Rendlesham Forest 87
Riches, William 52
Ringstead 149
Rochford 48
Rodney, Captain 95
Rolfe, Stephen 113, 114
Rowhedge 78
Rowlings, William 55
Rushley Island 53
Rushton, David 92

St Osyth Creek 65
Saffron Walden 31

Salcott 63
Sallowes, Sapperton 81
Sampson, John 69
Sayers, Captain John 127, 128
Sea Palling 133, 140
Seawick 66
Semer 116
Sheringham 33
Sherman, Thomas 54, 104
Shoeburyness 47
Sizewell Bay 97
Sizewell Gap 115, 122
Skeats, Joseph 159
Skipper Island 68
Snape 104, 124
South Benfleet 47
Southgate, Daniel 154
Southend 58
Southminster 48
Southwold 135
Southwold Custom House 107
South Woodham Ferrers 48
Spells, Edward 70
Stalham 140
Stanford-le-Hope 47
Stiffkey 147
Stiffkey Brook 131
Streaton, Thomas 71
Sudbury 68

Theberton 122, 123
Thetford, Robert 153
Thomas, Captain Richard 109
Thornham 147
Thornton, Mr 111
Thornton, 'Quids' 123
Thundersley 39
Thurgood, John 70
Thurrock 31
Thurston, Mr 37
Tibbenham, Tom 125
Tilbury 47
Tillingham 48
Tiptree Heath 63

Titchwell 147
Tollesbury 56
Turner, Captain John 100, 101
Turpin, Dick 48, 50

Unthank, John 111

Virley 63

Wadham-cum-Pallin 139
Walberswick 109
Wallasea Island 48, 55
Walton Backwaters 96
Walton on the Naze 67
Ward, John 81
Watson, Robert 105
Watson, William 81
Wayman, Samuel 113
Webb, William 154
Wells Custom House 152, 153
Wells-Next-The-Sea 147, 154
Weston Longville 15, 136
Wheatland, John 98
Whitaker Channel 51
Whitcomb, Mr 93
Whitehead, William 91
White Lyon Yard, Beccles 106
Wigboro Wick 66
Wigmore, Lambe 71
Willson, John 117
Wivenhoe 62, 76, 78
Wiseman, Mr 55
Wood, John 153
Woodbridge 87
Woodbridge Haven 96
Woodforde, Parson James 15, 43, 136, 139, 143, 163
Woodward, Captain James 79, 99
Wrestlers Inn, Yarmouth 127
Wright, William 56

Yarmouth 109, 112, 127
Yarmouth Custom House 111, 112